50 Fast Dreamweaver® MX Techniques

JANINE WARNER, IVONNE BERKOWITZ, AND
YANIER GONZALEZ

50 FAST DREAMWEAVER® MX TECHNIQUES

Wiley Publishing, Inc.

50 Fast Dreamweaver® MX Techniques

Published by
Wiley Publishing, Inc.
909 Third Avenue
New York, NY 10022

www.wiley.com

Library of Congress Control Number: 2003101787

ISBN: 0-7645-3894-2

Manufactured in the United States of America

10 9 8 7 6 5 4 3 2 1

1V/QX/QU/QT/IN

Published by Wiley Publishing, Inc., Indianapolis, Indiana
Published simultaneously in Canada

PREFACE

Web designers are always comparing notes with each other, studying the code behind Web pages they admire, and trying to figure out how to create the latest rollover effects, pop-up windows, and graphic elements that make a Web page come to life.

As three experienced Web designers, we've been playing this game for years, looking over the shoulders of our colleagues and sharing our best ideas with each other. In our 15+ years of combined experience as professional Web developers, instructors, and authors (including two other Dreamweaver books), we've collected far more than 50 great techniques, and we show you how to create the best ones in this exciting new book.

50 Fast Dreamweaver MX Techniques takes you way beyond Web Design 101 to show you how to quickly enhance your Web projects with the most sophisticated, visually captivating designs that are possible on the Web today. We also show you how Macromedia makes it easy for you to create these features with Dreamweaver. We included a few techniques related to Fireworks and Flash files because we want to help you get the most out these programs' integrated features. Whether you create your own Flash and Fireworks files, or just use Dreamweaver to pull everything together for your team, this book will help you take Web design to the next level.

In *50 Fast Dreamweaver MX Techniques*, you'll discover the hottest things you can do on the Web (the things other designers are always asking us to show them how we pulled them off). Each technique is fully illustrated and carefully described in step-by-step detail so that you can figure out how to use these cool features right away.

OVERVIEW OF THE TECHNIQUES

The 50 techniques detailed in this book are organized into 10 chapters. You can read them in any order and jump right into the ones that you are most interested in putting to use right away. As a general rule, the techniques do not build on each other, meaning you do not need to learn something from an earlier technique to be able to complete a later one. However, the first two chapters are designed to ease you into things (if that's your preference). Chapters 1 and 2 cover some of the simpler techniques so that you can enjoy instant gratification and pick up some of the basics (or get a quick refresher course) before you progress into the more complex techniques that make Dreamweaver such a powerful Web design tool.

As we've written these techniques, all three authors have drawn on real-world experience, including their favorite features and elements to show you how to create powerful features that really work on the Web today. We assume that you have some general knowledge of Dreamweaver, but within each section we explain everything you need to know to complete that technique and get it done fast. So dive into Chapter 1 or skip ahead to any chapter and get started right away on that cool feature you always wanted to add to your Web page.

WHAT COMPUTER HARDWARD AND SOFTWARE WILL YOU NEED?

FOR WINDOWS 9X, WINDOWS 2000, WINDOWS NT4 (WITH SP 4 OR LATER), WINDOWS ME, OR WINDOWS XP:

- PC with a Pentium processor running at 120 Mhz or faster
- At least 32 MB of total RAM installed on your computer; for best performance, we recommend at least 64 MB
- Ethernet network interface card (NIC) or modem with a speed of at least 28,800 bps
- A CD-ROM drive

FOR MACINTOSH:

- Mac OS computer with a 68040 or faster processor running OS 7.6 or later
- At least 32 MB of total RAM installed on your computer; for best performance, we recommend at least 64 MB
- A CD-ROM drive.

CONVENTIONS USED IN THIS BOOK

To make this book easy to use so that you can recreate the effects, we use a special format that focuses on the actual steps you need to take to complete the technique. Extraneous discussion is kept to a minimum.

We break each technique into major steps and explain what the step accomplishes. We refer you to the files on the CD-ROM you'll use in the technique. Follow the bullet points and figures to complete the technique on your own. Bold type designates items with which you interact and any text or numbers to be typed. Figure numbers also appear in bold type, as in **Figure 2.1**. If the figure is shown in the color section, the figure number includes a color plate number, such as **CP 2**, in parentheses, so that you can quickly find the image in color.

ACKNOWLEDGMENTS

Janine Warner

I have been graced by so many wonderfully supportive people that I can't possibly thank them all in any book — no publisher will give me enough pages for that. So I'll focus these acknowledgments on the people who made *this* book possible.

First, let me thank my extraordinarily talented co-authors, Ivonne Berkowitz and Yanier Gonzalez, who each deserve credit for a third of the techniques in this book. Ivonne is one of the most devoted cat owners I've ever met, and she deserves kudos for the design on my personal Web site, which people are always complimenting.

Ivonne, your innovative ideas, dedication to beating deadlines, and dogged attention to detail, make you an awesome coauthor. Thank you for everything.

Thanks also to Yanier, whose technical savvy is featured in some of the most advanced techniques in this book and whose creative designs help bring these pages to life.

Special thanks to our multi-talented editor Sarah Hellert, who helped keep track of us and all of the elements in this book (she should write a technique about how to do that). Sarah, your editor's eye always improves our work. Thank you.

Thanks to acquisitions editor, Mike Roney, for the great dinner in SF and for making this book happen in the first place. One of these days I'll make it to the "other" coast for dinner at your place.

Finally, I always like to thank my four fabulous parents Malinda, Janice, Robin, and Helen. And thank you, Daniel, for enriching my life with your music, wisdom, and precious love.

Ivonne Berkowitz

Above all, I have to say that my co-authors, Janine and Yanier were amazing once again. Janine, thanks for putting in the extra time to keep things organized and running smoothly! Believe me, the extra work has not gone unnoticed or unappreciated! Thank you for your friendship and encouragement — we miss you in Miami!

I am also grateful for all the help and support we've received from the editors. Mike, Sarah, and Mary, thanks for working so hard to get this book done on such a tight schedule!

Writing this book has been equal parts fun and madness. I'm touched and humbled by the amount of support I have received from the usual suspects and a quite few new ones: My parents, Emilio and Silvia, and my brothers, Emilio Jr. and George. My good friends Meredith, Caitlin, Jen, Rob, Ed, and Hugh, who live far away but are always close by in my heart. The gang at work, where it is always a pleasure to spend most of my waking hours every week: Scott, Rick, Alejandro, Maria, Patrick, Adam, Aislinn, Cathy, Louis, Ricardo, Pablo, Tilky, Christian K., Christian C., Ariel, Guillermo, Wendy, Paul, and Philip. My replacement, Stephanie, who has turned out to be a great friend as well. Jesus, Alfredo, Karina and Eddie, Vanessa; the Modernmethodites, including Robert, Raul, Tommy, James, and Veronica; Robbie Adams.

Yanier Gonzalez

First and foremost I'd like to thank Janine and Mike Roney. This was their baby, their vision — I was just a little piece of the puzzle. Thank you very much for your trust and terrific guidance. Ivonne – a big hug for anything and everything. Ivonne and Janine have helped me survive three books so far . . . I wouldn't dream of doing this again without you two. I'd also like to thank our amazing editor Sarah for mentoring me in the art of geek-speak removal and Mary for her *brutal* but extremely helpful input as a tech editor. Huge thanks to the powers at Wiley and Waterside for their support.

My involvement would not have been possible if it wasn't for the crew at ModernMethod. com. Thanks to Tlack, Rakool, James, Jahmon, Alan, and Vero for holding up the fort while I snuck out to play with Dreamweaver. Also, Marco.biz.org, Nice Will, Diego, Decha, Kallweb, Jesse fears Melinda, Franco loves DirtyG, Yosvany Rosello (frame this!), Miozzy, Frog&Fen, Jorge&Paco, the Monroys, Matias, Martins, and Walkers. I'd like to thank the companies whose sites grace our pages: Guzman & Company, Panexus, Ayesmides, Eliptek, Terespondo, Irie, Tracy, OscarG, BottomGrounds, and WWWorldmedia. I'll wrap this up with a family plug: Para Heri (Pa!), Mari, Lily&Julian, Oscar, Eli, Rey, Yoanka, Sarita (Ma!), the Duarte's, and the Berkowitz's. A very special thanks to Gabriel for pwawing. *Very off.* I may be a workaholic and rarely see you guys, but I'm thinking of you while I multi-task.

CONTENTS AT A GLANCE

CONTENTS

CHAPTER 3: THE TRICKS BEHIND ANIMATION TECHNIQUES 51

CHAPTER 4: CREATING POP-UP AND POP-UNDER WINDOWS 73

CHAPTER 6: DESIGNING FOR HIGH ACCESSIBILITY AND LOW BANDWIDTH 121

CHAPTER 7: IMAGE TRICKS THAT MAKE YOU LOOK GOOD   137

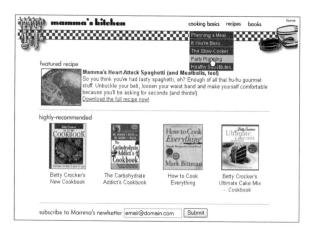

CHAPTER 8: TECHNIQUES TO SAVE YOU REPETITION 169

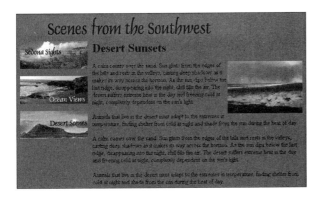

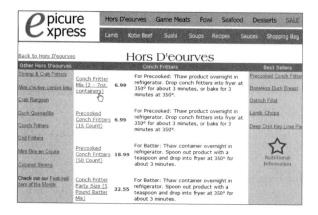

QUICK WAYS TO BRING YOUR SITE TO LIFE

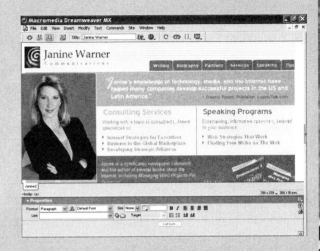

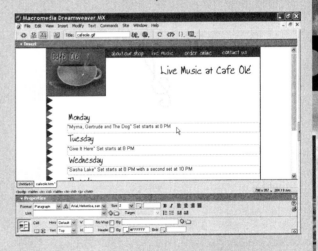

Y ou can create simple Web pages in any text-editing program, but Macromedia Dreamweaver offers features that can help you bring your site to life better than any other Web design program on the market. In this first chapter, I combine some of my favorite techniques to get you started. Follow the simple step-by-step instructions, and you'll be well on your way to creating compelling designs and making the most of your images.

If you're just starting to create a new Web page design, start with the Tracing Image feature in Technique 1. Tracing images are a great aid when you want to re-create a design in Dreamweaver that was first created in a program such as Photoshop or Fireworks. In Technique 2, you discover one of the most popular techniques in Dreamweaver, simple rollovers, which are ideal for Web site menus or navigation bars. Rollovers enable you to change the image when a user's cursor rolls over it. In Technique 3, you find out how to link one image to multiple destinations with Dreamweaver's image map tools. In Technique 4, you discover how well Dreamweaver is integrated with the Macromedia image-editing program, Fireworks, and how to import a design created in Fireworks into Dreamweaver. In Technique 5, you discover how best to display several big images by creating an image gallery of thumbnail images linked to larger images.

Tracing Images

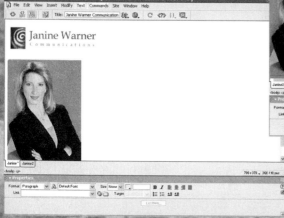

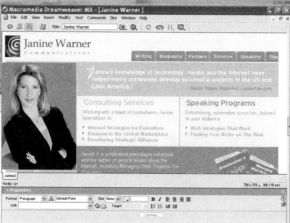

Rollovers

THE CONCEPT

THE CONCEPT

Image
Gallery Links

1

USING TRACING IMAGES
TO RE-CREATE DESIGNS

1.1 (CP 1)

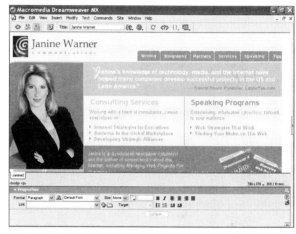

1.2 (CP 2)

NOTE

You can find all of the files used in this technique in the folder called Technique 1 on the CD-ROM.

Tracing images are a special feature in Dreamweaver that enable you to use a graphic to guide you as you build your page in Dreamweaver, much like you would put thin paper over a cartoon and re-create it by tracing over the cartoon on the paper.

Tracing images are a special Macromedia feature created to help you design your Web pages the way most experienced designers have found works best, by first mocking up the site design in an image program and then chopping it into pieces and re-creating it as a Web page in Dreamweaver.

Here's how it works. First, design your site in a program such as Photoshop or Fireworks, which enables you to have full design control while you're in the creative process. Then, you save your design as an image, which represents an entire page as it would appear on your Web site. This is your "mock up" image, which is great for getting the design the way you want it in a program like Photoshop, but won't work well on the Web where giant images take forever to download. To optimize your design for the Web, you need to build it with smaller GIFs, JPEGs, and other elements in Dreamweaver.

The brilliance of the tracing image comes in here. You can place this big image "behind" your page in Dreamweaver, as shown in **Figure 1.2 (CP 2)**. Then, use it as a guide as you re-create your design on top of it. You can position layers or create table cells on top of the tracing image, making it easier to exactly re-create your design in HTML. You can use JPG, GIF, or PNG format images as tracing images, and you can create them in any graphics application that supports these formats. In **Figure 1.1 (CP 1)** you see the same design being created on a blank page, without a tracing image to guide your work.

Tracing images are different from background images. Tracing images only appear in the Dreamweaver work area so that you can use them as you design your page. They will never be displayed in a browser, so your viewers will never see them on your site and you don't have to worry about what they look like or if they line up perfectly with your design. In contrast, background images become part of a page design and do display in a browser. You can use a tracing image and a background image on the same page.

STEP 1: INSERT A TRACING IMAGE

A tracing image should be a mock up of your page design, which you place behind a blank page in Dreamweaver so that you can re-create it with text, GIFs, JPEGs, and other elements in HTML.

- Open any existing page or create a new blank page in Dreamweaver by choosing **File ➢ New** and then **HTML Page**.
- Choose **View ➢ Tracing Image ➢ Load**.
- In the Select Image Source dialog box, select the image that you want to use as your tracing image and click **Select** to insert it behind the page.

TIP

If a tracing image doesn't appear, make sure that you have a check next to Show when you choose **View ➢ Tracing Image ➢ Show**.

(I used Tracing-Image.jpg from the Technique 1 folder.)

■ Alternatively, you can choose **Modify** ➢ **Page Properties** and use the **Browse** button next to the Tracing Image text box to select a tracing image.

■ Notice that the Tracing Image text box of the Page Properties dialog box displays the image name and its path.

■ Use the **Transparency** slider to set the opacity for the tracing image. This enables you to "soften" the tracing image so that you can more easily see the work you are doing on top of it. I set opacity to 45% in **Figure 1.3**.

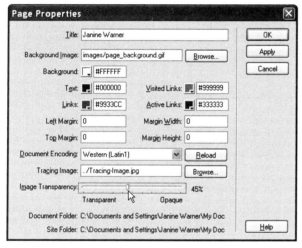

1.3

■ When you are done arranging the tracing image and have set the opacity the way you want it, click **OK**. The tracing image appears in the background of the document window.

TIP

Lowering the transparency level causes the tracing image to fade, making it easier to distinguish between the tracing image and editable elements on the page. You can set the transparency level to suit your preferences, but somewhere around 50% seems to work well with most images.

TIP

If you press **Return/Enter** without the **Shift** key, Dreamweaver inserts a `<p>` tag (paragraph), which puts a blank line between the logo and the photograph. Holding down the **Shift** key while you press **Return/Enter** inserts a `<br>` tag into the HTML and creates a single line break.

STEP 2: ARRANGE GIFS, JPEGS, AND OTHER ELEMENTS OVER THE TRACING IMAGE

With the tracing image in place, you're ready to re-create your design. You do this as you would create any page in Dreamweaver, but you have the advantage of having the tracing image as a guide behind your work.

- With the tracing image in place behind your page, choose **Insert ➤ Image** (see **Figure 1.4**), browse to find the image you want to use (I used logo.gif), and select it to insert it on the page. In this example, I placed the logo on the page and aligned it over the logo on the tracing image.
- Continuing with this design, choose **Insert ➤ Image** and select the photograph that goes below the logo (in the example, I used Janine.jpg). With the photograph still selected, use the left arrow key to move your cursor between the two images and then hold down the **Shift** key while you press **Return/Enter** to insert a line break. This positions

---

REMINDER

If a tracing image doesn't appear, make sure that you have a check next to Show when you choose **View ➤ Tracing Image ➤ Show**.

REMINDER

A tracing image doesn't replace a background image. The tracing image itself is visible only when you're editing the page in the document window; it never appears when the page is loaded into a browser.

Tag...	Ctrl+E
Image	Ctrl+Alt+I
Image Placeholder	
Interactive Images	▶
Media	▶
Table	Ctrl+Alt+T
Table Objects	▶
Layer	
Frames	▶
Template Objects	▶
Form	
Form Objects	▶
Email Link	
Hyperlink	
Named Anchor	Ctrl+Alt+A
Date	
Horizontal Rule	
Text Objects	▶
Script Objects	▶
Head Tags	▶
Special Characters	▶
Application Objects	▶
ASP Objects	▶
ASP.NET Objects	▶
ColdFusion Basic Objects	▶
ColdFusion Flow Objects	▶
ColdFusion Advanced Objects	▶
JSP Objects	▶
PHP Objects	▶
Get More Objects...	

1.4

the two images almost exactly over their corresponding images in the tracing image.

■ To re-create this entire page design, continue to place images, text, and other elements on the page. See **Figure 1.5**.

STEP 3: PREVIEW IN YOUR BROWSER

■ Press **F12** on your keyboard or click the **Preview in Browser** icon on the Document Toolbar.

■ The tracing image does not display in the browser.

OTHER TRACING IMAGE OPTIONS

You have a few other options with the Tracing Image feature. Choose **View ➤ Tracing Image** to reveal the following:

■ **Show:** Hides the tracing image if you want to check your work without it being visible but don't

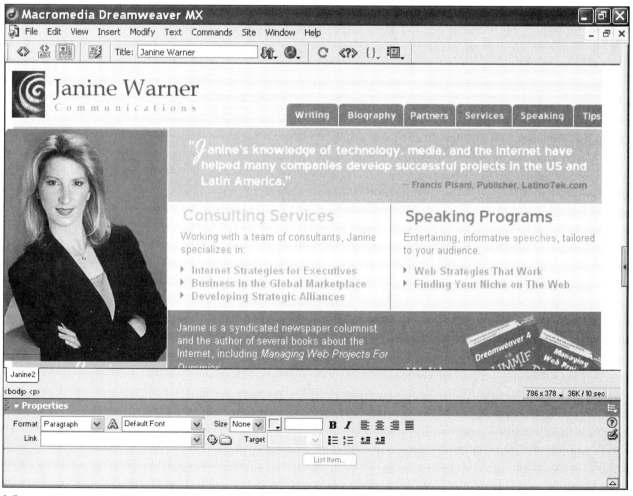

1.5

want to remove it. You need to uncheck Show for the tracing image not to appear in Dreamweaver.

■ **Align with Selection:** Enables you to automatically line up the tracing image with a selected element on a page.

■ **Adjust Position:** Enables you to use the arrow keys or enter X, Y coordinates to control the position of the tracing image behind the page.

■ **Reset Position:** Resets the tracing image to 0, 0 on the X, Y coordinates.

CREATING ROLLOVERS
FOR INTERACTIVITY

2.1 (CP 3)

2.2 (CP 4)

NOTE

You can find all of the files
used in this technique in the
folder called Technique 2 on
the CD-ROM.

One of the most popular places to use rollover effects is
on a Web site's menu buttons. As shown in **Figures 2.1
(CP 3)** and **2.2 (CP 4)**, rollovers call attention to particular items, visually letting a user know when an item is a
link, for example. You can also use rollovers to provide
additional information when the mouse is placed on a particular item on
the page.

A rollover is comprised of a set of two (or more) images and a JavaScript
behavior. In a simple rollover, there are usually two images: the "off" state
and the "on" state. For example, you may create menu items that contain
black text on a white background for the "off" state and red text on a white
background for the "on" state. If the rollover behavior is properly applied,
the text looks like it is changing color from black to red when the cursor is
placed over it.

STEP 1: INSERT AN IMAGE AND DEFINE PROPERTIES

■ Choose **File ➤ Open** and browse to find the file called Technique2.htm for this technique. This page has already been built for you with the basic images in place to maintain proper spacing.

■ Click the word **Concept** at the top of the page to select the image RTConcept_off.jpg. Delete this image.

■ Choose **Insert ➤ Interactive Images ➤ Rollover Image** to display the Insert Rollover Image dialog box.

■ Enter the following in the fields of the Insert Rollover Image dialog box, as shown in **Figure 2.3**.

■ Name the image in the Image Name text box.

■ In the Original Image text box, type the name of the image, RTConcept_off.jpg, that is first seen on the page. This is the image to which the rollover action will be applied. You can also use the **Browse** button to select the image.

■ In the Rollover Image text box, type the name of the image, RTConcept_on.jpg, that replaces the original image when you place your mouse over it.

■ Leave Preload Rollover Image checked if you want your rollover images to load when the page loads. This ensures that a user won't have to wait with his or her mouse over the original image while the rollover image loads.

■ Enter descriptive Alternate Text that appears while the original image is loading.

■ Enter a URL or a Web page name in the When Clicked, Go To URL text box if you want this rollover image to be a link.

■ Click **OK**.

STEP 2: CONFIRM AND TEST

■ Click **File ➤ Preview in Browser** and select a browser or press **F12** on your keyboard if you have already set up a shortcut to a browser for testing and previewing.

■ The page you are working on opens in a browser window.

■ Place your mouse over the image to test that the rollover works correctly, as shown in **Figure 2.4**.

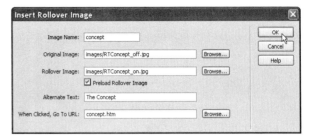

2.3

2.4

SETTING LINKS IN AN IMAGE MAP

3.1 (CP 5)

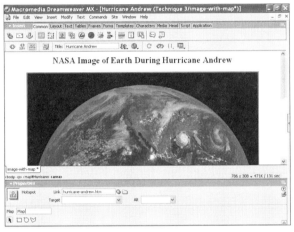

3.2 (CP 6)

Image maps, such as the one shown in **Figure 3.2 (CP 6)**, enable you to link different sections of the same image to different pages. Image maps are used to make single images doorways into multiple places. Image maps are popular on the Web because they enable you to create hot spots in an image and link them to different URLs or Web pages. A common use of an image map is a geographic map, such as a map of the Earth shown in this example. Each of the hot spots in Figure 3.2 (CP 6) links to a different page that highlights the damage done by Hurricane Andrew.

Image maps have many uses. For example, if you own a chain of music stores in California and want to make it easy for customers to find a local store, you can create hot spots on an image map of California and then link each hot spot to a page listing stores in that geographic location or linking directly to a page for the store.

Dreamweaver makes creating image maps easy by providing a set of simple drawing tools that enable you to create hot spots and specify their corresponding links.

13

STEP 1: INSERT AN IMAGE AND OPEN IMAGE MAP TOOLS

You create an image map by first inserting an image on a page as you would insert any image. Then, using Dreamweaver image map tools, you click and drag to create hot spots over different areas of the image. Each hot spot can be linked to a different URL.

Follow these directions to create an image map:

- Create a new blank page in Dreamweaver by choosing **File ➢ New** and selecting **Basic Page** and **HTML**. Choose **Insert ➢ Image** or click the **Image** icon in the Common Tools panel. Browse to find the earth.jpg image in the Technique 3 folder.
- Alternatively, you can open the file Technique3.htm in the Technique 3 folder. This file has the image already placed on a page.
- If the Property inspector isn't already visible, choose **Window ➢ Properties** to open it.

- Notice that when you select the image, the options in the Property inspector change to represent image options. If it's not already expanded, click the small arrow in the bottom-right corner of the Property inspector to reveal all of the image options, as shown in **Figure 3.3**. (The Image map tools are only available when the Property inspector is expanded.)

STEP 2: CREATE HOT SPOTS ON AN IMAGE MAP

You can specify the regions in an image map by using three Shape tools:

- **Rectangular Hotspot Tool:** Creates a rectangular area over an image that you can link to another page.
- **Oval Hotspot Tool:** Creates an oval area over an image that you can link to another page.

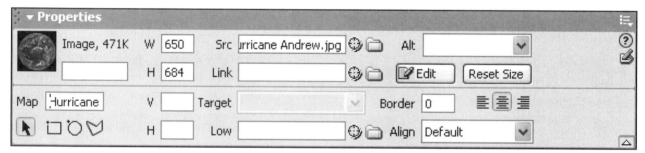

3.3

- **Polygon Hotspot Tool:** Creates a custom shape over an image. To make a polygon selection (such as one over the state of Florida in the example), click the tool once for each point of the polygon shape you want to draw. Then, to close the shape, click again on the first point you drew after you finish drawing all the other points.
- Click the **Shape** tool you want from the Property inspector, and then click and drag on the image to create a hot spot. In this example, I used the Oval tool to create hot spots over the hurricane and over the other tropical storm area, as shown in **Figure 3.4**.
- To create a hot spot in an unusual shape, such as the hot spot over Florida in this example, click the **Polygon** tool and then click and draw around the outline of the area you want to make hot, ending at the original point to complete the hot area.

- To reposition a hot spot or change its size, click the **Arrow** tool from the Property inspector. To resize a hot spot, click any of the small resize handles at the edge of the image and drag to the desired size. To reposition, click in the middle of the hot spot and drag to move the entire hot area.

STEP 3: SET LINKS IN AN IMAGE MAP

- Click to select a hot spot and then click in the Link text box in the Property inspector.
- Type the URL to which you want the hot spot to link.
- You can also use the Browse button, the small folder icon to the right of the Link text box in the Property inspector. Click the **Browse** button and navigate to find the page to which you want to link. Click to select the page and then click **OK**. The path and page name appear automatically in the Link text box.

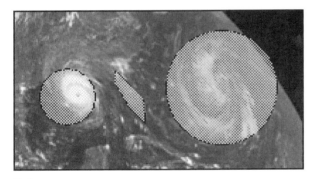

3.4

REMINDER

You can go back at any time and change the links in an image map by clicking the blue region that indicates a hot spot and entering a new URL.

EXPORTING A LAYOUT FROM FIREWORKS INTO DREAMWEAVER

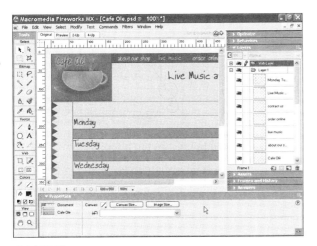

4.1 (CP 7)

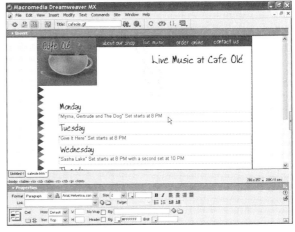

4.2 (CP 8)

Many designers use Fireworks and Dreamweaver together, creating a layout image in Fireworks and then exporting it to a file that can be easily integrated into a site created in Dreamweaver. In **Figure 4.1** (**CP 7**), you see a layout as it appears in Fireworks before it's exported. In **Figure 4.2** (**CP 8**), you see the same layout as it appears in Dreamweaver.

Exporting from Fireworks to Dreamweaver is a timesaving solution if you prefer to do your design work in a graphics-editing program, such as Fireworks and don't want to manually slice it into pieces and then reassemble it in Dreamweaver. A more complex layout may require some tweaking after you export it to HTML, but more often than not, the time you save is significant.

I provide a sample Fireworks file on the CD-ROM called Technique4.png. However, you can create your original layout in Photoshop or Fireworks. If you create a layout in Photoshop, simply open the .psd file in Fireworks and proceed from there.

STEP 1: SLICE YOUR LAYOUT FOR OPTIMUM FILE SIZE

- In Fireworks, select the **Slice** tool.
- "Slice" your layout into small pieces. Position the crosshair cursor where you want to begin your slice and then click and drag diagonally to complete the slice. Each slice is highlighted in green by default. **Figure 4.3** shows the logo in the upper-left highlighted. Repeat this step until you have sliced the entire layout.

Some slicing hints: When slicing a layout, it's a good idea to keep areas with similar colors together as a slice or set of slices. For a menu, select the entire area that you want to see as a button on your finished page. Finally, try to run the slices edge to edge with each other. If you leave spaces between one slice and another, Fireworks creates many tiny default slices.

STEP 2: OPTIMIZE EACH SLICE

Optimizing each slice ensures the fastest load time possible for your Web page.

4.3

- Click a slice.
- In the Fireworks Property inspector, choose the type of slice you want to use: Image or HTML. If this slice does not contain an image, you can choose **HTML** from the Type menu. If it is an image, choose **Image** and then the most appropriate type of optimization (GIF, JPEG, and so on), as shown in **Figure 4.4**.

STEP 3: EXPORT TO HTML

As soon as you determine properties for all your slices, you can export the entire layout to HTML.

- Click **File ➤ Export**. The Export dialog box appears, as shown in **Figure 4.5**.
- Browse to find the directory in which you want to save your new HTML page.
- Give your page a name, such as technique4.htm, for example.
- Save as type: **HTML and Images**.
- HTML: **Export HTML File**.
- Slices: **Export Slices**.
- You can also determine if you want to export only some specific slices or areas without slices instead of the entire layout. This is handy when you've already exported the entire layout before, and just want to update the content of one slice.

> **TIP**
>
> You can turn off the Slice Overlay view by using the **Show Slices** toggle button, located under the Slice Tool button, or by clicking the eye icon next to the first layer, the Web Layer, in the Layers palette.

- If you want to save your images to a subfolder, check **Put Images in Subfolder** and click to browse for the appropriate folder. Otherwise, leave this option unchecked.
- Click **Save**.

4.5

STEP 4: OPEN THE HTML PAGE IN DREAMWEAVER

Now you can view the new HTML file in Dreamweaver and make any necessary changes.

- In Dreamweaver, click **File ➢ Open** to browse for the new page. The completed file is in the Technique 4 folder. It is named technique 4.htm.
- Select the file and click **Open**. As you can see, your layout looks just as you created it in Fireworks. Each slice is now its own image within the HTML layout, as shown in **Figure 4.6**.

TIP

When slicing a layout, try to keep parts of the layout that contain a gradient together as one slice or a set of slices, and set the optimization for those slices to **.jpeg** in the Optimize panel. Slices containing solid colors or a combination of colors with no gradients can be optimized in .gif format. You can preview the quality of an optimized slice by clicking the **Preview** tab at the top of the image file. Fireworks displays your layout the way it will look after optimization has been performed. Play with the different optimization settings to get familiar with the results on different parts of the layout.

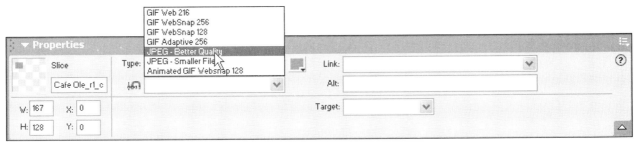

4.4

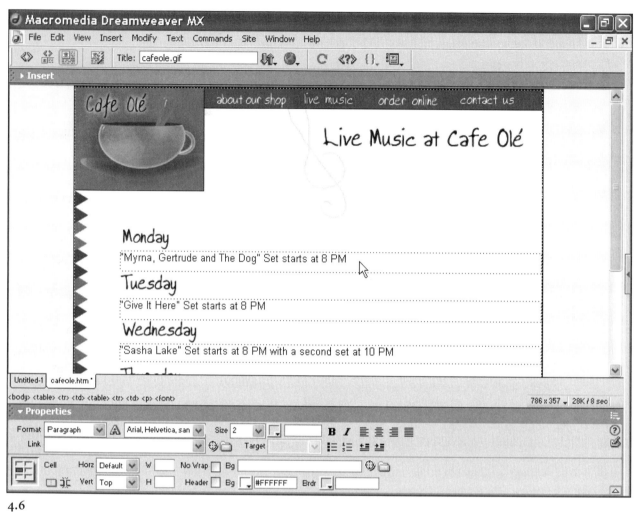

4.6

CREATING A LINKED IMAGE GALLERY

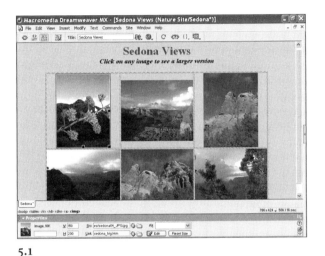

5.1

5.2

A linked image gallery, such as the one shown in **Figure 5.2**, is an ideal way to display multiple images on one page. Because of long download times and the limited display area on a computer screen, placing too many large images on one page is problematic. Instead, try arranging several smaller images on a page and then linking them to larger versions of the same images, each on its own page.

In this example, photographs of Sedona are displayed as small images on the main page with links to larger images, each on its own page that includes descriptions and other information.

STEP 1: CREATE AN IMAGE GALLERY

You can use a linked image gallery for any collection of images, from paintings to photographs to clip art. Follow these instructions to place your images on a page and link them to other pages.

■ Open any existing page or create a new blank page in Dreamweaver by choosing **File ➢ New** and then **Basic Page** and **HTML Page**.

■ Choose **Insert ➢ Table** and specify the number of columns and rows. In this example, I created a table that is two rows by three columns so that I could place each of the photos I took in Sedona in its own table cell.

■ Click to insert your cursor in the first table cell, choose **Insert ➢ Image**, browse to find the image you want to use, and select it to insert it in the table cell.

■ Click to insert your cursor in the second table cell, choose **Insert ➢ Image**, browse to find the image you want to use, and select it to insert it in the table cell.

■ Continue inserting the thumbnail images until all of the small images are in their own cells in the table.

STEP 2: SET LINKS FROM THE IMAGE GALLERY TO LARGER IMAGE PAGES

Before you can link the small images to their corresponding pages, you need to create those pages. By that I mean creating a separate HTML page for each larger version of the image so that you can link the smaller images to the HTML page that contains the

larger image. Then, create a page that displays all of the smaller images and set links from the smaller images to the pages that contain the larger images.

■ Click to select the first thumbnail image (see **Figure 5.3**) and then use the **Browse** button (the small folder icon to the right of the Link text box in the Property inspector) to locate the page to which you want to link. In **Figure 5.4**, I'm setting the link to the first thumbnail.

■ Repeat this for each small image. See **Figure 5.5** for the finished Web page.

5.3

5.4

REMINDER

You don't have to create a table when you create an image gallery, but it is an excellent way to organize images and control the spacing around them.

5.5

CHAPTER 2

TIMESAVING TECHNIQUES YOU CAN USE TODAY

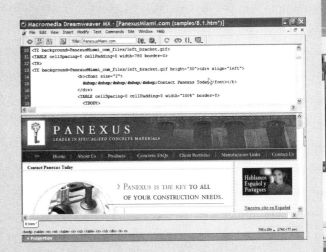

Building and maintaining a Web site can be an extraordinarily time-consuming project. When I first started building Web sites, everything had to be done manually, from writing HTML code to fixing broken links and organizing the files and folders that make up a site's structure. When Dreamweaver came on the market, I was excited because I immediately saw the timesaving benefits of this great program. Now, several years and a few upgrades later, Dreamweaver is a comprehensive program with a broad range of features designed to save you time and make Web design easier than ever before.

In this chapter, you find some of Dreamweaver's most valuable and timesaving techniques, from automatically finding and fixing broken links to developing a template-driven site. You also find out how to clean up cluttered code, gain quick access to site assets, and how to organize your files and folders without breaking any links.

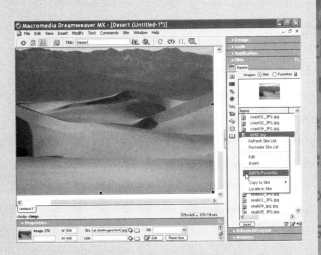

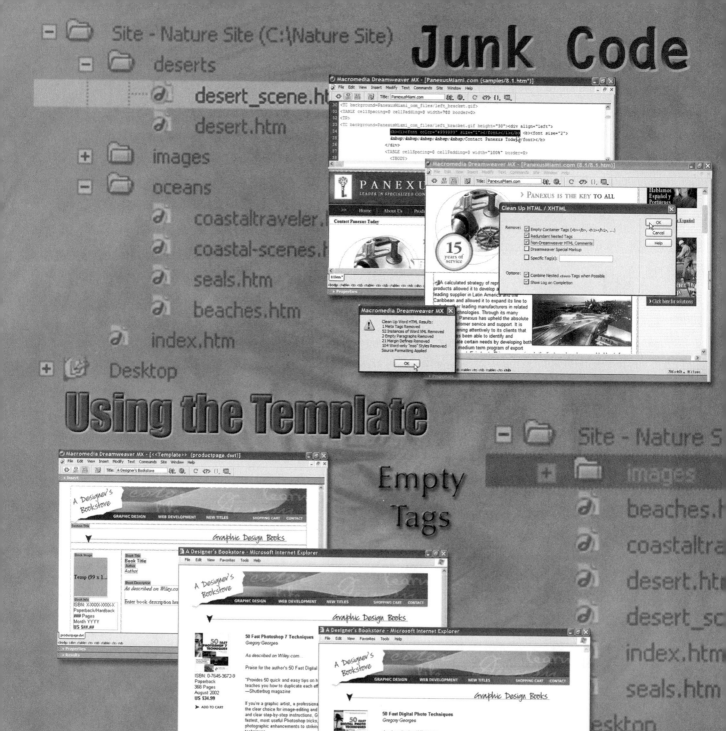

FINDING AND FIXING BROKEN LINKS AUTOMATICALLY

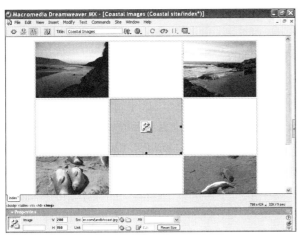

6.1 (CP 9)

6.2 (CP 10)

The broken link on this page of nature photos is easy to fix with Dreamweaver's link checking feature.

Broken links are one of the most embarrassing problems you can have on a Web site. Links can get broken so easily: Just move a file, change a filename, or link to another Web site that disappears, and you have a broken link. Broken links become especially problematic as a Web site grows and gets more complex.

Nothing can turn your users off faster than coming upon a page with a broken image link, such as the one shown in **Figure 6.1 (CP 9)** or clicking a link and getting a "File Not Found" error page (also known as a "404 error" because that's usually the message viewers see if they click a broken link). Fortunately, Dreamweaver offers a few features designed to help you find and fix broken links, even on large, complex Web sites.

STEP 1: FIND BROKEN LINKS

Before you can fix a broken link, you have to identify that it's broken. Some links, such as the broken image link shown in Figure 6.1 (CP 9) are easy to spot, but broken links to other pages can go unnoticed if you don't test your links regularly yourself. Follow these steps to use the Dreamweaver Link Checking feature to easily identify broken links in a page or Web site.

- Make sure the site you want to work on is selected and that you have at least one page of the site open in the Dreamweaver work area. You can do this by selecting the site name from the pull-down menu at the top of the Site panel and choosing the site you want to work on from the list.
- From the Site panel, choose **Site ➢ Check Links Sitewide** (see **Figure 6.3**). You can also check the links on a single page by opening that page and choosing **File ➢ Check Links**.

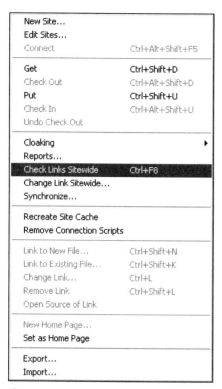

6.3

- Whether you check a single page or the entire site, the Check Links Results panel opens at the bottom of the page, just under the Property inspector, as shown in **Figure 6.4**. The dialog box displays a list of filenames with broken links, as well as any pages, images, or other items that are not linked to any other pages in the site. This is handy if you want to clean up old images or other elements that you are no longer using on the site.

STEP 2: FIX BROKEN LINKS

As soon as you identify which links are broken, you are anxious to fix them. Dreamweaver enables you to correct broken links right from the Link Checker Results panel. Simply identify the correct link, and Dreamweaver automatically fixes it for you.

After using the Link Checker, described in the preceding step, to identify broken links, follow these steps to use the Results panel to fix them.

> **TIP**
>
> If you like keyboard shortcuts, use ⌘/**Ctrl+F8** to Check Links Sitewide and ⌘/**Ctrl+F8** to Check Links on the page you are viewing

> **TIP**
>
> You can save the Link Checker's report by clicking the **Save Report** button (the small floppy disk on the left-hand side) in the Link Checker panel. This is handy if you want to be able to refer to it later, print it out, or share it with someone else who works on your Web site.

■ With the Results panel open at the bottom of the page, double-click a filename that Dreamweaver has identified as a broken link to open the page and its corresponding Property inspector. The Results panel should remain visible. (If you are checking the links on a single page, you can skip this step.)

■ In the Results panel, click to select a broken link or broken image, and then click the folder icon to the right of the filename.

> **WARNING**
>
> The link checking only works in local mode, on a local site. A broken link that is external (i.e., to an image or page that is outside the main folder of your site, such as a file on another Web site) cannot be identified by Dreamweaver's Link Checker. Dreamweaver does help you identify potentially broken links by creating a list of external links that appear in the selected document or Web site.

■ Navigate to find the page or image file to which the link should go, click to select it, and then click **OK**. The link is automatically fixed. If it was a broken image link, the image reappears in the work area, as shown in **Figure 6.5**. If it was a broken page link, when you preview the page in a browser, the link works.

■ If you already know the location of the file to which you want to link, you can type the correct filename and path in the File name text box or browse to find the image. The correct image must be in a folder that is accessible to the site's root folder.

■ You fix links to pages just like you fix links to images, except you type the name of the correct file into the Link text box or click the **Browse** button next to it to find the file in your site folder.

■ If you are fixing a link to a page on another Web site, you must enter the URL manually in the link SRC text box of the Property inspector.

■ If the link that you correct appears on multiple pages, Dreamweaver prompts you with a dialog box asking if you want to fix the remaining broken link references to the file. Click **Yes** to automatically correct all other references. Click **No** to leave other files unchanged.

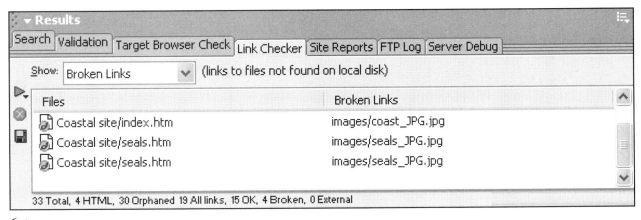

6.4

6.5

CREATING A TEMPLATE-BASED WEB SITE

7.1 (CP 11)

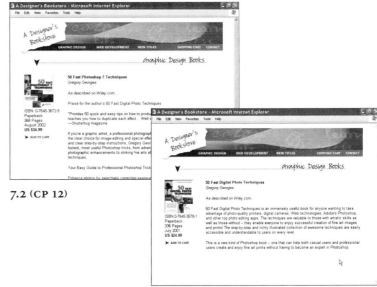

7.2 (CP 12)

7.3 (CP 13)

Working with templates can save you a lot of time if you have to create many pages with the same elements. **Figure 7.1 (CP 11)** shows the template used to create the Web pages shown in **Figures 7.2 (CP 12)** and **7.3 (CP 13)**. Not only does working with templates speed up the page creation process, but also, when the time comes to make changes to some of the elements that appear on every page, you only have to make those changes once.

To follow through with this technique, you can use the sample page on the CD-ROM referred to here or create your own page to use as a template. I use the sample page here, which was created by using Fireworks and Dreamweaver.

STEP 1: PREPARE THE PAGE TO SERVE AS A TEMPLATE

- Choose **File ➢ Open** and browse to find Technique7.htm.
- Choose **File ➢ Save As Template**. The Save As Template dialog box appears.
- Click to select your local site from the list.
- Enter a name for your template and click **Save**. See **Figure 7.4**. Dreamweaver saves your template with a file extension of .dwt, and automatically

NOTE

You must already have defined a local site in Dreamweaver in order to create templates for it.

TIP

After you create a template file, you can access it at any time through the Assets panel. Choose **Window ➢ Assets** to open the panel, and then click the Templates icon to see all of the templates associated with this site. See also Technique 9, "Accessing URLs, Colors, and Images Assets."

creates a folder called Templates in your local site directory to store this and any other templates you create for this site.

STEP 2: DEFINE EDITABLE REGIONS

Editable regions are the areas of template-based pages that you can change on the "child" pages created from the template. Locked regions are only editable on the template master page, which has a filename that ends in .dwt.

- On your template, click to select an area you want to make editable. I selected the section title graphic — the part that includes "Graphic Design Books" — because I want to be able to change this graphic title depending on the section of the site on which I'm working.
- Choose **Insert ➢ Template Objects ➢ Editable Region**. The New Editable Region dialog box appears. Enter a name for this editable region and click **OK**. See **Figure 7.5**.

TIP

If you've selected a region but don't see the colored box or the region name, choose **View ➢ Visual Aids** on the main menu. The choice Invisible Elements should be checked.

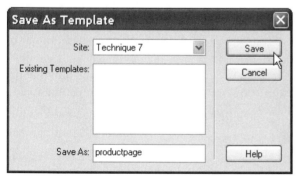

7·4

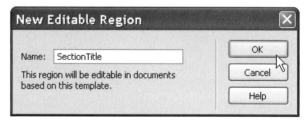

7·5

■ The selected region now appears inside a colored box, with the region name on the top-left corner. See **Figure 7.6**.

■ Follow these steps for every region you want to make editable on your template. See **Figure 7.7** for an example of a finished template.

■ Choose **File ➤ Save**.

STEP 3: CREATE A PAGE USING THE TEMPLATE

Now that you defined your template, or master page, you can create any number of pages based on this template.

NOTE

Notice that the graphic header and menu area is not defined as an editable region. That means this area is locked to users editing the template-based pages. You should only define as editable regions parts that will change from page to page. You should keep locked such features as navigation, header logo, or graphics and copyright information.

■ Open a new page in your site by choosing (⌘/**Ctrl+N**). Click the **Templates** tab, highlight your site and the template name that you want to use (in this case, productpage), and click **Create**. Then save the page using **As**. Enter the page name, including .htm at the end; otherwise, Dreamweaver will not open it later on.

■ Choose **Modify ➤ Templates ➤ Apply Template to Page**. Select the template named productpage from the list and click **Select**. The template's content appears on this new page. A yellow border and tab let you know this page is attached to the template named productpage. The

---

NOTE

You can make text region editable by selecting the cell in which you want to be able to add or edit text. Select the cell by clicking the appropriate `<td>` tag at the bottom of the screen. When the cell is selected, you can follow Step 2 to make it an editable region.

7.6

7.7

editable regions are highlighted in blue as they were in the template master page. The menu appears locked when you place your mouse cursor over it. See **Figure 7.8**.

■ Type the content into the editable regions and insert images into any region that requires an image. See **Figure 7.9**.

■ Follow these steps to create as many template-based pages as needed.

STEP 4: EDIT THE TEMPLATE AND UPDATE ALL PAGES

If you make any changes to the template file, Dreamweaver will update all attached pages in one easy step.

■ Open the template productpage.dwt.

■ Change the link on the "Contact Us" menu graphic from contact.htm to contactus.htm.

TIP

If you decide later that you don't want the template to be attached to a certain page, you can easily detach the template by clicking **Modify ➢ Templates ➢ Detach from Template**. The page loses all template properties and become a regular HTML document. All regions that were previously locked become fully editable.

■ Choose **File ➢ Save**. The Update Template Files dialog box appears, listing all the pages that are attached to this template. If you want to update all files, click **Update**. To update only some files, select the files you want to update and then click **Update**. See **Figure 7.10**.

7.9

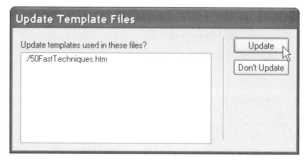

7.10

7.8

8

REMOVING EMPTY TAGS AND JUNK CODE

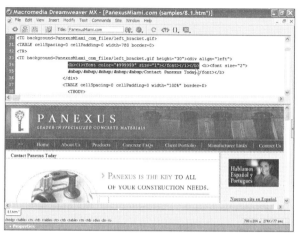

8.1

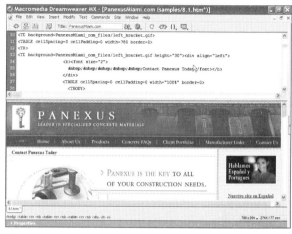

8.2

> **NOTE**
>
> You can find all of the files used in this technique in the folder called Technique 8 on the CD-ROM.

Virtually all visual Web design programs have a tendency to litter your document with unnecessary code, as shown in **Figure 8.1**. It's the price you pay for the push-click convenience they offer. While usually harmless, junk code and empty tags can often cause unwanted white space, unpredictable formatting of images and text, as well as larger file sizes. This junk code doesn't contribute anything to your Web site, and it also makes your code harder to read.

Unwanted code appears for a number of reasons. If you're editing formatted text and moving blocks of text around, you may unintentionally produce empty font tags or bold/italic tags. This is most likely to happen if you primarily use the Design View mode to build your Web pages because your eyes are not immediately on the code. You can flip to Code View and remove these tags by hand, but this is time-consuming. Luckily, Dreamweaver MX comes packed with powerful tools to assist you in cleaning up this unwanted code in a matter of clicks without compromising the integrity of your Web pages, as shown in **Figure 8.2**.

STEP 1: MAKE A BACKUP VERSION

Backing up your work is a good idea before you dabble with this technique, just in case the cleanup tools remove code that you want to keep.

- Choose **File** ➢ **Save As** (⌘/Ctrl+Shift+S) to save a new copy of your document. Give the new document a different name and click **Save**.

STEP 2: SPECIFY THE CLEANUP TYPE

Dreamweaver MX offers two automated code cleaning utilities: Clean Up HTML and Clean Up Word HTML. Both commands offer slightly different features, which are outlined here. If your file was created with Microsoft Word, run the Clean Up Word HTML command first.

NOTE

Junk tags aren't limited to Dreamweaver MX. If you converted a Microsoft Word document into an HTML file, you'll find a library of unique (and often unnecessary) tags. Software by Adobe usually leaves behind comments containing name and version numbers of its software.

TIP

The Clean Up Word HTML command also works wonders on other Microsoft Office products, including HTML files generated by PowerPoint, Excel, and Access.

- Choose **Commands** ➢ **Clean Up HTML**.
- The Clean Up HTML/XHTML dialog box, shown in **Figure 8.3**, appears with the most common options already selected.
- You can turn on three additional code-cleansing features by checking **Non-Dreamweaver HTML Comments**, **Dreamweaver Special Markup**, or **Specific Tag(s)**. When you specify tags, keep in mind that Dreamweaver removes every instance of that tag — not just the unwanted ones. Keep Show Log on Completion checked to see the results of the command immediately.
- Alternatively, choose **Commands** ➢ **Clean Up Word HTML**.
- The Clean Up Word HTML dialog box (see **Figure 8.4**) displays two tabs: Basic and Detailed. Click the **Basic** tab, and you find most of the features from the Clean Up HTML menu, plus two unique options: Remove All Word Specific Markup and Clean Up CSS. Click the **Detailed** tab to reveal various parameters for both of these options.
- Choose the version of Word that created this document from the Clean Up HTML menu, as shown in Figure 8.4.

8.3

■ Check **Remove all Word Specific Markup** to remove HTML tags that contain Word-specific XML, VB Script code (if/then tags), and original Word formatting tags.

NOTE

When removing CSS, your fonts will usually be affected, and the positioning of images and paragraphs may shift.

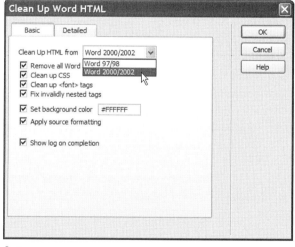

8.4

■ Check **Clean up CSS** to remove style sheets generated by Microsoft Word.

TIP

You can save yourself a lot of work by saving Word files as "HTML filtered," which reduces the amount of Word-specific markup, although it still leaves a fair share. If you intend to continue editing a document in Microsoft Word, these tags may be necessary to keep.

TIP

A standard set of styles is generated with every Word HTML document — styles that specify the font size, how paragraphs are spaced, how bullets appear, and so forth. There are often as many as 30 styles defined even if your document has no formatting and consists of only one sentence. These tags, which usually start with MSO, can be removed safely and replaced with more efficient formatting by using Dreamweaver MX's Styles or traditional style sheets.

STEP 3: INITIATE THE CLEAN UP

- Within the dialog box, select the check boxes that best fit your filtering criteria. Click **OK** to execute the Clean Up HTML command.
- A log appears showing you how many tags were removed and consolidated. Click **OK** to close the log. See **Figure 8.5**.

The cleanup is now complete. You may find your document dramatically changed or not changed at all — this is all contingent on how much "junk" there was initially and how many cleaning options you chose. If the cleanup produced unwanted results,

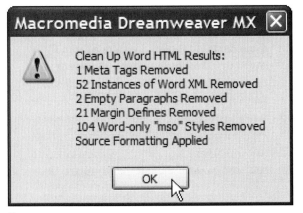

8.5

simply choose **Edit ➤ Undo** (⌘**/Ctrl+Z**) to move back one step. You can repeat this process without consequence as long as you don't save your document.

In some cases, the Cleanup HTML commands miss certain tags, markup, or CSS references. You can take various steps to remove these additional tags. Your best do-it-yourself utility is the search-and-replace option found under the Edit menu. You can specify an unwanted tag, its parameters, and have it removed by leaving the "replace" field blank. Of course, you can also switch to Code View, highlight the unwanted tags, and use your trusty delete key. Just remember that tags open and close, so hunt them down in pairs and check back in Design View on a regular basis to make sure you didn't remove anything important. Dreamweaver MX highlights orphan tags in yellow if you miss any.

If you are working on Web pages with a programmer, be cautious when applying these commands to pages containing custom code. While Dreamweaver MX may find incomplete or redundant tags, this is often done on purpose (especially if conditional loops, such as if/then statements, exist on the page). Even if the file seems to work after you run these commands, it's wise to save a copy of the original prior to cleaning the file of unwanted tags. Of course, you can always ask your programmer to clean the code for you while you move on to the next technique!

9

ACCESSING URLS, COLORS, AND IMAGES ASSETS

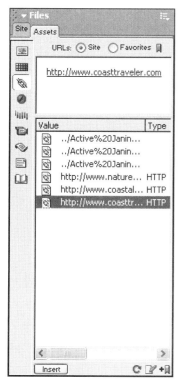

9.1 (CP 14)

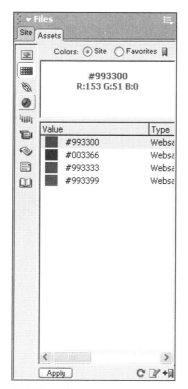

9.2 (CP 15)

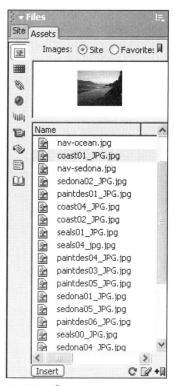

9.3 (CP 16)

The Assets panel boasts many great features, including easy access to the URLs, Colors, and Images panels, shown in **Figures 9.1 (CP 14)**, **9.2 (CP 15)**, and **9.3 (CP 16)**, respectively. Dreamweaver automatically collects every image, link, and color you use in your site and stores references to them in these handy asset panels where they are easy to access when you want to add any of these elements to your pages.

Each Assets panel has two display options, one that lists every element and another where you can specify your favorites. For example, if you add the images you use more frequently to the Favorites list, you won't have to search through a list of every image on your site when you want to use them.

STEP 1: USING IMAGES ASSETS

Dreamweaver automatically stores all of the images in the folders in your site in the Images Assets panel, where you can apply them to your pages with drag and drop ease. The other advantage of the Images Assets panel is that it provides a thumbnail preview of each image, so if you're trying to remember what you called an image, you get a reminder in the preview area at the top of the Images Assets panel, as shown in **Figure 9.4**. To use the Images Assets panel, follow these steps.

■ Click the **Assets** tab from the Files panel group in the panels that appear in the right of the Dreamweaver work area. Then, click the **Images** icon at the top-left of the Assets panel. The images in your site appear in a list in the main area of the Images panel.
■ You can reorder images by filename by clicking **Name**, by size by clicking **Size**, and by file type by clicking **Type**.
■ To insert an image on a page, simply open the page in the main work area of Dreamweaver, click the filename in the Images Assets panel, and drag

it onto the page. Dreamweaver automatically inserts the image on the page. You can then change the attributes of the image in the Property inspector.

■ To add an image to the Favorites section of the Images Assets panel, right-click the image name and choose **Add to Favorites**, as shown in Figure 9.4.

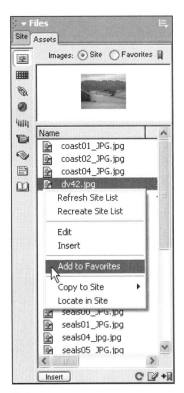

9.4

STEP 2: ADD COLOR ASSETS

When you apply a color to text or links on your pages, Dreamweaver automatically stores those colors in the Colors Assets panel. The beauty of this is that you don't have to remember exactly what color you used when you want to apply it to another element: You can simply open the Colors Assets panel and drag it from the list onto the page.

To apply a previously used color to text on a page by using the Colors Assets panel, follow these steps.

- Click the **Assets** tab from the Files panel group in the panels that appear in the right of the Dreamweaver work area. Then, click the Colors icon, second down in the row at the top left of the Assets panel. The Colors panel opens, and all of the colors used in your site appear in a list in the main area of the Colors panel.

> ### TIP
>
> If you don't see all of your images or other elements in the Assets panel, click the **Refresh** icon (the circular arrow) at the bottom right of the Assets panel. If you still don't see all of your assets, try exiting Dreamweaver and then starting the program again. When you add new elements, Dreamweaver needs to restart to "find" them and include them in the Assets panel.

- To apply a color to text on a page, simply open the page in the main work area of Dreamweaver, highlight the text or link to which you want to apply the color, click the color name in the Colors panel, and drag it onto the text in the work area. Dreamweaver automatically inserts the color onto the page. You can then change the attributes of the color in the Property inspector. (**Figure 9.5** shows the Colors panel with a color applied to text on a page.)
- To add a color to the Favorites section of the Colors Assets panel, right-click the color and choose **Add to Favorites**.

STEP 3: APPLY URL ASSETS

One of the most convenient features of the Assets panel is the automatic collection of URLs. This is especially useful for external links because it can save

> ### WARNING
>
> If you use CSS to specify color and then you apply a color from the Assets panel, it will override the style sheet. You should only do this if you're sure you want to use a special color that is distinct from your style sheet. Of course, if you don't use CSS, you don't have to worry about this.

9.5

your having to look up addresses when you want to link to the same place again. Every time you create a link in your Web site, Dreamweaver automatically stores the URL in the URLs Asset panel. To apply a URL to a page by using the URLs Asset panel, follow these steps.

■ Click the **Assets** tab from the Files panel group in the panels that appear in the right of the Dreamweaver work area. Then, click the URLs icon, which looks like a chain link and is third down in the row at the top left of the Assets panel. The URLs panel opens, and all of the URLs used

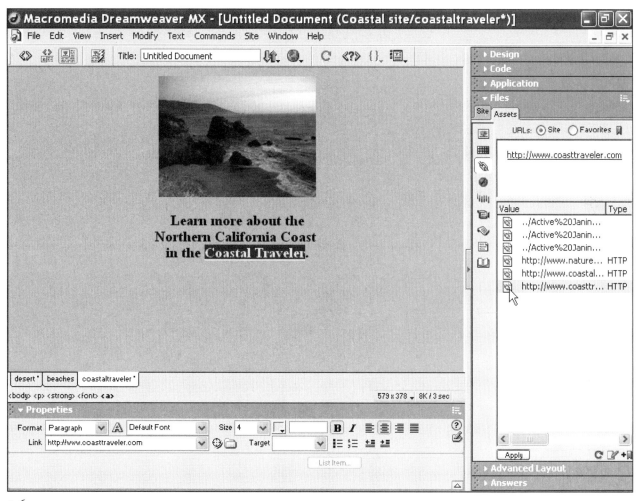

9.6

in your site appear in a list in the main area of the URLs panel.

■ To apply a URL to an element, such as text or an image on a page, open the page in the main work area of Dreamweaver, highlight the text or link to which you want to apply the URL, click the URL in the URLs panel, and drag it onto the text

or image in the work area. You can also click the **Apply** button at the bottom of the Assets panel. Dreamweaver automatically creates the link, as shown in **Figure 9.6**.

■ To add an URL to the Favorites section of the URLs Assets panel, right-click the URL and choose **Add to Favorites**.

ORGANIZING FILES AND FOLDERS WITHOUT BREAKING LINKS

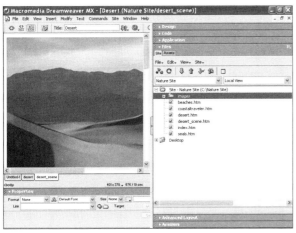

10.1 (CP 17)

10.2 (CP 18)

Dreamweaver's Site panel is a wonderful timesaver because it automatically adjusts links when files are moved in a Web site, as shown in **Figures 10.1 (CP 17)** and **10.2 (CP 18)**.

As Web sites grow, they can get increasingly complicated to manage. Many Web designers start by putting all of the main files in a site in one folder. Then, one day they realize that it's getting hard to find the file they want to work on because they have one really long list of files in one folder. That's the day they think, hey, I'll just create some new folders and move files into them to organize the site. But the files in a Web site can't just be moved around like the files on your hard drive, because they are all interconnected with links that get broken if you move them around by using the system options on your computer.

That's where Dreamweaver's Site panel becomes an incredible timesaver. If you create new folders or move files around by using the Site panel, Dreamweaver automatically fixes any corresponding links.

STEP 1: SET UP A WEB SITE

Before you use Dreamweaver's site management features, you have to set up your site in Dreamweaver. This preliminary step should be done before you start doing any work on a Web site, but because it's crucial to being able to use the features described in this technique, you find instructions for setting up a site in the following steps. If you have already set up your site, skip ahead to Step 2, Create New Folders.

To set up a Web site in Dreamweaver, follow these steps.

- Click the **Site** tab from the Files panel in the panels that appear in the right of the Dreamweaver work area.
- From the pull-down menu in the top left of the Site panel, choose **Edit Sites**. In the Edit Sites dialog box that appears, choose **New**.
- In the Site Definition dialog box, shown in **Figure 10.3**, enter a name for your site next to Site Name. You can call your site anything you want. This name appears only in the list of sites in Dreamweaver's Site panel and is used to help you distinguish between sites if you use Dreamweaver to manage multiple sites.
- Click the **Browse** button to the right of the Local Root Folder field in the Site Definition dialog box, shown in Figure 10.3, and navigate your hard drive until you find the folder that contains your Web site. Click the name of the folder and then click **Select**. (If you use the example included on the CD, you should select the folder called "Disorganized site.")

REMINDER

Keep all of the files and folders that make up your Web site in one main folder on your hard drive. That way, when you transfer the files to a Web server, you can keep all of your files in the same relative location, meaning they stay in the same place relative to each other — a crucial element in keeping links functional.

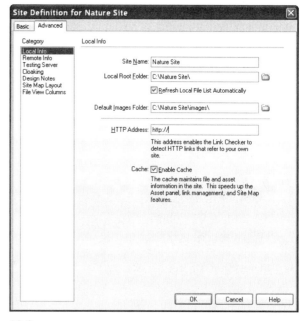

10.3

■ Click the **Browse** button to the right of the Default Images Folder field in the Site Definition dialog box, shown in Figure 10.3, and navigate your hard drive until you find the folder that contains the images in your Web site. Click the name of the folder and then click **Select**. If you use multiple folders for your images, you can skip this step or select the folder that holds the most images. Dreamweaver assumes the folder you select is where your image files are located unless you specify otherwise.

■ Specify the URL if you have a domain set up for your site. Make sure the **Enable Cache** box is checked and click **OK**.

The other options listed under Category, including Remote Info, are not required to use the site management features described in this technique but are necessary if you want to use other Dreamweaver features, such as FTP capabilities, which enable you to transfer your files to a Web server.

STEP 2: CREATE NEW FOLDERS

Before you can start organizing a growing site, you want to create new folders, and you want to do that in the Site panel so that Dreamweaver can help you keep track of these folders and the files you will move into them.

In the sample site used in this technique, you see a simple Web site with all of its files in the main folder of the site, as shown in **Figure 10.4**. You can organize the

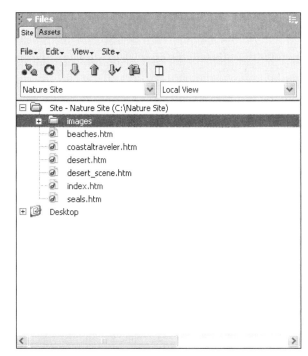

10.4

site by adding folders and moving the files into subfolders. This is a great step to take when you expect your site to grow and you want to create folders for related pages so that they are easier to find in the future. You can use Dreamweaver's site management features with a small site, such as the one shown in this example, as well as with a much larger site.

To create new folders in a Web site, follow these steps:

- Click the **Site** tab from the Files panel group and make sure the Site pull-down menu specifies the site on which you want to work. Also make sure that the main folder of your site is selected (highlighted) in the main area of the Site panel.
- From the Site panel (not the main menu) choose **File ➤ New Folder**, as shown in **Figure 10.5**, and then name the folder.

TIP

Before you start making significant changes to a Web site, such as creating new folders and moving files around, it's always a good idea to save a backup copy of the entire site.

- To create additional folders, choose **File ➤ New Folder**, as shown in Figure 10.5, and then name the folder.

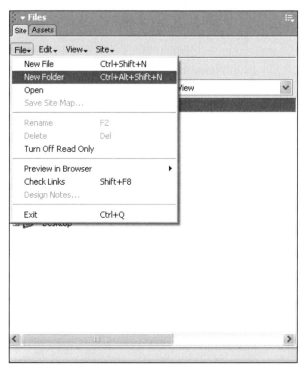

10.5

STEP 3: MOVE FILES INTO NEW OR DIFFERENT FOLDERS

In the sample site shown in this technique, I created separate folders for the pictures of the ocean and the pictures of the desert. The next step is to move files into those folders to organize the site, as shown in **Figure 10.6**.

Follow these steps to move files into folders and automatically adjust any related links.

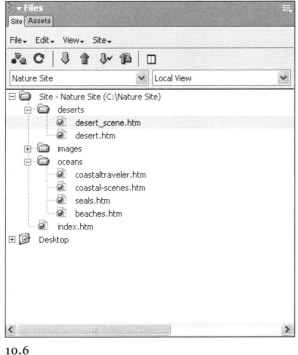

10.6

■ Click the **Site** tab from the Files panel group and make sure the Site pull-down menu specifies the site on which you want to work.

■ Click to select a file in the Files panel and move it by dragging it onto a folder name. The Update Files dialog box opens, as shown in **Figure 10.7**, asking if you want to update related links. Click **Update** to adjust the links as you move the file and ensure that you don't break any of the links as you move files into new or different folders. If you don't choose Update, then when the file is moved you will break the links from any other files that link to it.

■ You can use the sample site provided on the CD-ROM in the folder Technique 10 to experiment with moving files. Simply drag files from one folder to another, or create new folders and move files into those to see how Dreamweaver automatically fixes broken links.

10.7

CHAPTER 3

THE TRICKS BEHIND ANIMATION TECHNIQUES

I t's true. You don't *always* need Macromedia Flash to create animation and movement effects on the Web. Dreamweaver offers a variety of features designed to add movement and action to your Web site.

Rollover Behavior

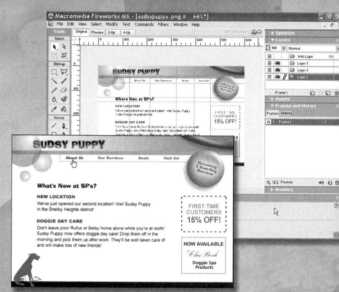

Flash movies

Triggers

SWAP IMAGE

CREATING A DISJOINTED (ONE-TO-MANY) ROLLOVER EFFECT

11.1

11.2

NOTE

You can find this page, named Technique11.htm, on the CD-ROM.

Disjointed rollovers follow the same concept as simple rollovers, except that the image affected or changed by the rollover is not necessarily, or exclusively, the one on which the mouse is placed. In **Figure 11.1**, for example, a graphical menu is on the left side of the page, and an empty space is in the center of the page. When you mouse over each menu item, a full image pertaining to that menu item replaces the empty space (see **Figure 11.2**). Behind the scenes, this is what's really happening: There is a default blank image in the center (I call this the "off" state). When you create the rollovers, instead of applying the behavior to the image on which you place your mouse, you apply it to the default, or "off" state, image on the center of the page.

You can also use simple and disjointed rollovers simultaneously for added interactivity. For example, when designing a navigation menu for your Web site, you can add a simple rollover to the menu item, at the same time adding a disjointed rollover so that an image elsewhere on the page changes depending on where the mouse is on the navigation menu.

STEP 1: INSERT THE TRIGGER IMAGE

The trigger image is the image that when "touched" by the cursor *triggers* the rollover effect.

- Open the file named Technique11.htm from the Technique 11 folder on the CD. The trigger images (the three CD covers on the left side) have already been inserted for you. If you are working on one of your own pages, perform the following steps to insert your trigger images.
- Position your cursor where you want to insert the image.
- Choose **Insert ➤ Image** or click the **Image** icon in the Insert bar. You can also insert an image from the Assets panel, as described in Technique 9, "Accessing URLs, Colors, and Images Assets."
- Browse for an image to insert.
- Select the image.
- Click **OK**.

STEP 2: INSERT THE IMAGE THAT WILL BE AFFECTED BY THE ROLLOVER

The base image is the image that will be replaced when the cursor rolls over the *trigger* image. The disjoint image (RTDisplayblank.gif) has already been inserted into the center part of Technique11.htm for you.

- If you are working on one of your own pages, repeat the instructions in Step 1 to insert the image.
- In the Property inspector, give each image a unique name, as shown in **Figure 11.3**.

STEP 3: SET THE SWAP IMAGE BEHAVIOR

- Click the image that triggers the rollover effect.
- With the image selected, click the **Behaviors** tab in the Design panel group.

11.3

- Click the **Plus Sign** (+) button.
- Choose **Swap Images** from the pull-down menu. The Swap Image dialog box appears. See **Figure 11.4**.
- From the Images list, choose the image that will be affected by the rollover (the image that will change). In Technique11.htm, this image is named display.
- Click **Browse** to select the image you want to use as the rollover image.
- Click **OK**.

TIP

In the Swap Image dialog box, check **Preload Images** to ensure that all your rollover images are loaded when the page is loaded into the browser. This reduces or completely eliminates the amount of time a user waits for the images to download. Check **Restore Images onMouseOut** to return your rollover image to its original state when the mouse is moved away from the trigger image.

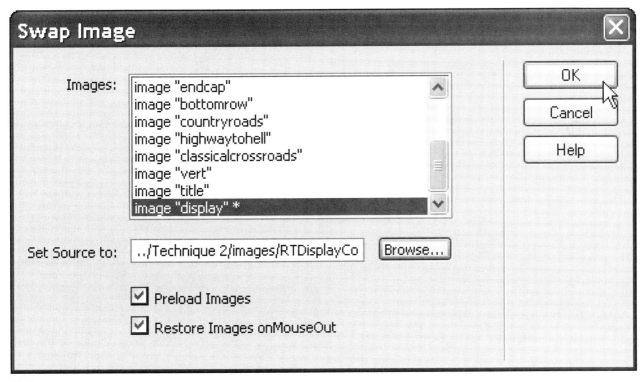

11.4

- Click **OK**. The newly created behavior appears in the Design panel, under the Behaviors tab. See **Figure 11.5**.

11.5

STEP 4: PREVIEW IN YOUR BROWSER

- Press **F12** on your keyboard or click the **Preview in Browser** icon on the Document Toolbar. See **Figure 11.6**.

11.6

BUILDING ROLLOVERS IN FIREWORKS AND EXPORTING THEM TO DREAMWEAVER

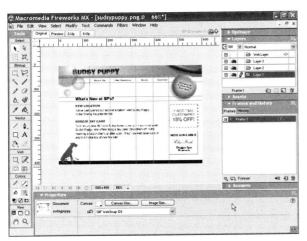

12.1 (CP 19)

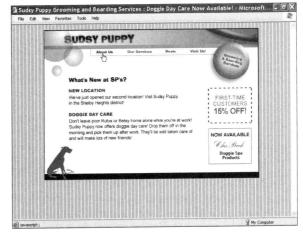

12.2 (CP 20)

If you're using Fireworks to design your layout, you can create the rollover behavior in Fireworks, as shown in **Figure 12.1 (CP 19)**. instead of doing it later in Dreamweaver. In this technique, you discover a quick and easy way to build rollovers in Fireworks and export both the graphics and the code.

STEP 1: CREATE THE ROLLOVER FRAME

After you open Technique12.png in Fireworks, notice that all the layers are in Frame 1. You create the rollover effect — what you want your rollover to look like — in Frame 2.

■ In the Frames and History panel, click the Panel Options **menu** icon on the right. From the menu, choose **Duplicate Frame**. Choose **After current frame** from the dialog box and click **OK**. Frame 2 appears in the Frames and History panel, as shown in **Figure 12.3**.

■ On Frame 2, select the menu text (**About Us, Our Services, Deals, Visit Us**). With all the menu text items selected, change the color of the text by using the Property inspector. I used #CC0000 as my rollover color.

STEP 2: ADD THE ROLLOVER BEHAVIOR

Now that you have created the frame for your rollovers, add a rollover behavior to each menu item.

■ Make sure that you are back on Frame 1 in the Frames panel and that the Web Layer is visible in the Layers panel so that you can see the layout slices. If the Web Layer is invisible, click the layer. An eye icon appears to the left of the layer name to let you know that it is now visible, as shown in **Figure 12.4**.

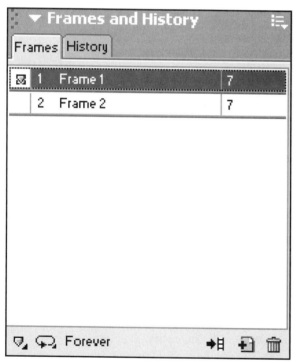

12.3

■ Click the slice covering the **About Us text** to select it. A white circle icon appears in the center of the slice.

■ Click the circle to view a menu of available behaviors. Choose **Add Simple Rollover** from the menu, as shown in **Figure 12.5**. The new behavior appears in the Behaviors panel on the right side of your screen. If the Behaviors panel is not visible, choose **Window ➤ Behaviors** or press **Shift+F3** to open the panel. Perform this step on the remaining menu items.

STEP 3: EXPORT THE LAYOUT TO HTML AND OPEN IN DREAMWEAVER

After you add the rollover behavior to all your menu buttons and make any other final changes to the layout, you are ready to export to HTML. (Before exporting, the image slices need to be optimized.

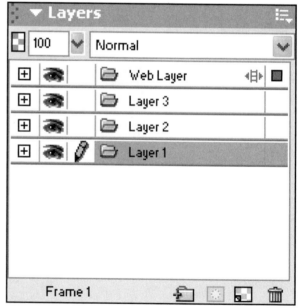

12.4

See Step 2 of Technique 4, "Exporting a Layout from Fireworks into Dreamweaver.")

■ Choose **File ➢ Export** or press **Ctrl+Shift+R**. The Export dialog box appears.

■ Click the **Browse** button to find the directory in which you want to store the HTML page and its corresponding images. By default, your HTML page is given the same name as your .png file. You can give it a different name in the File Name field.

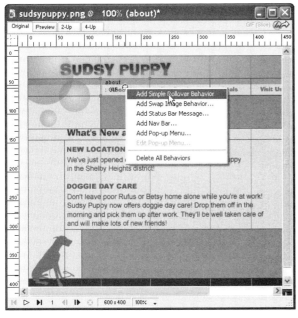

12.5

If you want to export the images into an image subdirectory, you can specify the directory by checking **Put Images in Subfolder** and then browsing for the folder in which you want to save your images.

■ Click **Save**.

■ Open the new HTML file in Dreamweaver. You can see the rollover behaviors by clicking the menu button images. The behavior for each button appears in the Behaviors panel.

■ As soon as you have the page open in Dreamweaver, you can make changes to the HTML and layout, such as adding a page background, centering the layout on the page, or adding a page title. You can also copy the desired portion of HTML from this page and place it into another HTML page.

■ Preview your finished page in a browser by pressing **F12** on your keyboard. See **Figure 12.6**.

NOTE

You can preview the page in a browser before exporting to Dreamweaver by choosing **File ➢ Preview** in your browser or by pressing **F12**.

12.6

EMBEDDING A FLASH MOVIE

13.1

NOTE

You can find all of the files used in this technique in the folder called Technique 13 on the CD-ROM.

Embedding rich interactive content from Macromedia Flash is one of the most effective ways to make your static pages come to life. You can make your Flash movie appear to be transparent, control the rendering quality, and manage the dimensions and alignment of the movie on the page. There are various parameters, or properties, to consider when embedding a Flash movie on the page that go far beyond just inserting the Flash file. **Figure 13.1** shows a Web page with an embedded Flash movie.

STEP 1: INSERT THE FLASH MOVIE

- Open the file called Technique13.htm and click inside the area in your Web page where you want to insert the Flash file. This can be anywhere in the body of the page or inside a table cell.

- Choose **Insert ➤ Media ➤ Flash** (**Ctrl+Alt+F**) or click the **Flash** icon in the Insert bar. See **Figure 13.2**. The Insert Flash dialog box appears.
- Browse to find presentation.swf. Click **OK** to insert.

STEP 2: MODIFY THE PARAMETERS

When Dreamweaver inserts a Flash movie on a Web page, some HTML and ActiveX code is inserted into the document. If you inspect the code, you'll find two seemingly identical instructions on how to display the movie. These OBJECT and EMBED tags in these

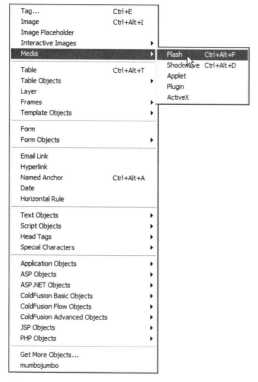

13.2

instructions ensure that various types of browsers can view the movie. You also find the Dreamweaver inserts the URL where you can find the Flash version's plug-in, which triggers an auto-install if you don't have it.

```
<OBJECT classid="clsid:D27CDB6E-AE6D-
11cf-96B8-444553540000" codebase=
"http://active.macromedia.com/flash2/
cabs/swflash.cab#version=4,0,0,0"
WIDTH=100% HEIGHT=600>

<PARAM NAME=movie VALUE="og.swf">
<PARAM NAME=quality VALUE=high>
<PARAM NAME=bgcolor VALUE=#39484F>

<EMBED src="og.swf" quality=high
bgcolor=#39484F  WIDTH=100% HEIGHT=600
TYPE="application/x-shockwave-flash"
PLUGINSPAGE="http://www.macromedia.com
/shockwave/download/index.cgi?
P1_Prod_Version=ShockwaveFlash">
</EMBED>

</OBJECT>
```

> **TIP**
>
> Flash comes with a built-in HTML generating feature that can do some of the work for you. It generates the EMBED and OBJECT tags, sets the background color of the body to the Flash movie's background, and gives you limited alignment and quality control. Please refer to the help files that come with your Macromedia Flash application for more information.

Interestingly enough, Dreamweaver does not treat the three PARAM tags (shown previously) and a few others (Play and Loop, for example) as actual parameters: They are not shown in the Parameters dialog box. By clicking the inserted Flash movie, you find that these three PARAM tags have individual check boxes in the Property inspector. You can access the Parameters dialog box by selecting the Flash movie in your document in Dreamweaver and clicking the Parameters button in the Property inspector.

- Click the inserted Flash movie. Your Property inspector shows Flash movie properties.
- Check or uncheck the **AutoPlay** and **Loop** check boxes for the desired effect. These parameters are defaults in Flash, so even though they don't exist in the code, they are checked in Dreamweaver. If you uncheck them, Dreamweaver inserts the following code:

NOTE

While Parameters are powerful, they have their limitations. The AutoPlay and Loop parameters cannot control the animation of movie clips within your Flash movie — they only control the progression of the main timeline. Also, the WMODE parameter makes only your Flash movie's background transparent. If you create solid shapes or use an unmasked photo as a background instead, the Flash file will not appear transparent because of layer overlap within your movie. The Quality parameter does not affect the quality of your imported raster graphics (such as JPG and GIF) within the Flash movie — those values are determined when you create the SWF with Flash.

```
<param name="LOOP" value="false">
<param name="PLAY" value="false">
```

- Set the quality of the movie by making a selection in the Quality box. Choosing **High** makes your Flash file look its best.
- Set the background color of the Flash file. In most cases, Dreamweaver attempts to fill in this Hex value for you.
- If you want to add transparency or other parameters to your movie, click the **Parameters** button on the right side of the Property inspector. The Parameters dialog box appears (see **Figure 13.3**).

REMINDER

Flash files are not literally embedded into Web pages. They are simply referenced by the EMBED and OBJECT tags. The external SWF file is called upon and controlled by these tags and the parameters described. Also, be wary of the Edit button on the Property inspector. In some cases, this button opens the SWF as a static frame-by-frame animation. This may not be the original FLA source file you used to create the Flash movie. The Edit button is better reserved for Dreamweaver-made Flash files (see Technique 15).

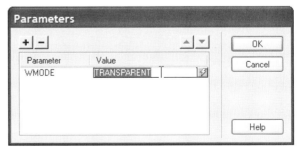

13.3

■ Enter the parameter name on the left side and its value on the right side. For a transparency effect, set Window Mode (WMODE) to **Transparent**.

■ Click **OK**. Save and test your Web page.

Your Flash movie is now properly embedded into your Web page. See **Figure 13.4**.

13.4

EMBEDDING A MULTIMEDIA FILE

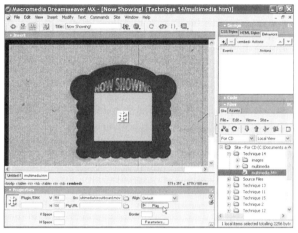

14.1 (CP 21)

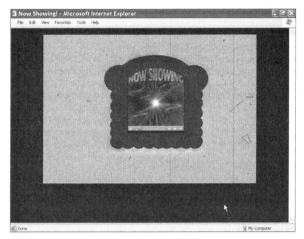

14.2 (CP 22)

Whether you're a videographer who wants to showcase work samples, or a family guy who wants to share home movies of grandchildren, embedding multimedia files, such as QuickTime movies into your HTML page is painless using Dreamweaver. **Figure 14.1 (CP 21)** shows a multimedia file embedded into a Web page. **Figure 14.2 (CP 22)** shows the multimedia file playing on a Web site.

STEP 1: CREATE THE PAGE THAT CONTAINS THE MULTIMEDIA FILE

- Open the file called Technique14.htm in the Technique 14 folder on the CD-ROM.
- Or, create a page, leaving a space for your movie.

STEP 2: INSERT THE CODE THAT EMBEDS YOUR MULTIMEDIA FILE

■ Place the cursor where you want to embed the file.

■ Choose **Insert ➣ Media ➣ Plugin**. Browse for the file you want to embed. (I used circuitboard. mov from the multimedia subfolder in the Technique 14 folder.) Click to select it and then click **OK**. A plug-in icon appears, as shown in **Figure 14.3**.

14.3

■ Change the W and H values in the Property inspector to resize the icon to the size you want your movie to be when it plays. You should know this size beforehand. Entering a size other than the movie's actual width and height causes the movie to distort when it plays. The movie on the CD-ROM plays 159 pixels wide and 130 pixels high, so resize the plug-in icon to those dimensions, as shown in **Figure 14.4**.

Unlike the HTML code for an embedded Flash movie, the HTML code for this QuickTime movie looks a lot simpler:

> **NOTE**
>
> When thinking about placing multimedia files within your Web pages, you should also consider the size of those files. Sometimes multimedia files are large and take a significant amount of time to download. If you know that most of your target audience is using a DSL connection or faster, a 2MB file isn't a problem. However, that isn't the case when the majority of your audience is using a dial-up connection. Many dial-up users will not wait the time it takes to download that 2MB file at such a slow speed.

```
<embed src="multimedia/
circuitboard.mov" width="159"
height="130"></embed>
```

STEP 3: TEST YOUR MULTIMEDIA FILE

■ Now that your multimedia file is embedded, click the **Play** button on Dreamweaver's Property inspector (see Figure 14.4). The movie begins playing in the document window, as shown in **Figure 14.5**.

REMINDER

Not all users can view the contents of your multimedia file. Some users' browsers don't support the file type, for example. In some cases, the user lacks the plug-in. Dreamweaver allows you to enter a URL to the plug-in download Web site in the Plug-in URL text box in the Property inspector. If the plug-in isn't installed, the user will be prompted to visit that Web site to download and install it.

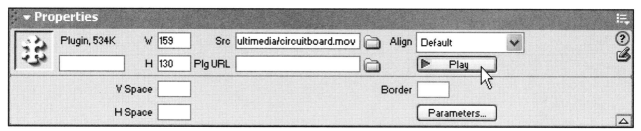

14.4

14.5

CREATING A FLASH MENU
IN DREAMWEAVER

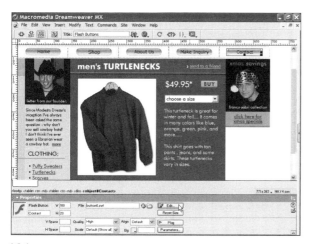

15.1

15.2

Y ou don't always need to dive into Macromedia Flash to create interactive buttons for your site. The Dreamweaver Interactive Images menu enables you to pick and choose from a wide variety of premade buttons, readily available to customize and insert into your Web pages, as shown in **Figures 15.1** and **15.2**.

STEP 1: PREPARE YOUR SITE

■ Copy the Technique 15 folder from the CD. Remove the read-only designation if required. Make sure that all of the files are in the same site, and that the site is defined in Dreamweaver

STEP 2: FIND A STYLE THAT SUITS YOUR DESIGN

- Save your Web page. The Interactive Images feature generates SWF files for your buttons, so it needs to know where to deposit them (relative to your pages).
- Click the area in your Web page where you want each button to appear. I've included each button in an individual cell in a table, as shown in **Figure 15.3**.
- Choose **Insert ➢ Interactive Images ➢ Flash Button**. The Insert Flash Button dialog box appears.
- A preview of a button style appears at the top of the dialog box. Use the Style scrollbar to find more designs. Click the style you want to use (see **Figure 15.4**).

STEP 3: SPECIFY WHAT THE BUTTON DOES

Unlike normal image buttons, Flash buttons contain the URL, Window Target, and other information within the SWF file. This means that these items won't appear on your Property inspector after the file is generated — instead you find Flash parameters (refer to Technique 13, "Embedding a Flash Movie"). There are no required fields.

- Enter the button text to display in the Flash button.
- Choose a font from the menu for your button. Choose your font size by entering the size in points. The default point size is 12.
- Enter the URL in the Link text box or click the **Browse** button to locate the file to which you want to link. Select a Target as needed.

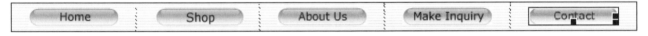

15.3

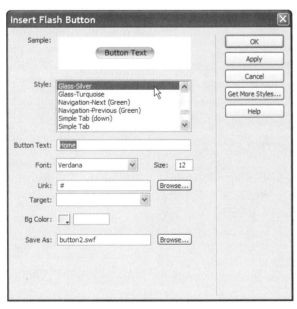

15.4

TIP

You can download more button styles and templates from the Macromedia Exchange. Choose the Interactive Images menu and in the Insert Flash dialog box, click the **Get More Styles** button to be directed to Macromedia's site. To learn more about add-ons, please refer to Chapter 10, "Extend the Features of Dreamweaver with Extensions."

■ Enter the background color you want to see behind the button. Most styles have a solid white background — the shapes are not masked to transparent by default. Please refer to Step 2 of Technique 13, "Embedding a Flash Movie," for instructions on how to specify transparent background parameters in Flash.

■ Enter a filename for the Flash movie. Click the **Browse** button to save the SWF file in a different directory.

■ Click **OK** to render the button. See **Figure 15.5**.

■ Click the **Edit** button on the right side of the Property inspector to call back the Insert Flash

Button dialog box if you want to modify these specifications at a later time. See **Figure 15.6**.

Your Flash button is ready and working. Dreamweaver inserts all of the necessary code to properly embed the button in its place, as well as the plug-in code. For more information on manipulating embedded Flash files, please see Technique 13. For the completed Web page, see **Figure 15.7**.

REMINDER

You can edit the buttons you create (choose a new model, change the text, and so forth) by clicking them and clicking the **Edit** button in the Property inspector. However, you cannot change the look of the button in Flash.

15.5

15.6

15.7

CHAPTER 4

CREATING POP-UP AND POP-UNDER WINDOWS

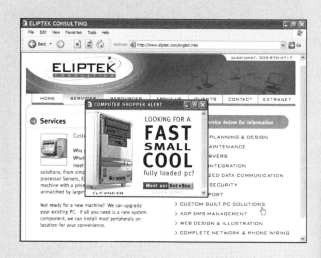

L ove them or hate them, there's no doubt that pop-up and pop-under windows are popular on the Web today. This chapter shows you how to create pop-up and pop-under windows — the notorious, miniature Web pages frequently used to display small amounts of information and, increasingly, to deliver advertisements on top of or just behind Web pages.

Pop-up windows are essentially normal HTML Web pages, which are resized on the fly by JavaScript. Using a combination of Dreamweaver MX behaviors, you can spawn pop-up and pop-under windows after visitors click a button, roll over a picture, or exit your Web site. You also explore how to create the new generation of pop-ups — the type you can't just close — using DHTML behaviors. Pop-under windows work much the same way, except that instead of appearing above a Web page, they appear behind it, becoming visible after a user closes the main browser window.

Warning: There are valid reasons to use pop-ups, but not all of your visitors can see them. Not everyone likes these little windows, especially because they are most commonly used for advertising. Some programmers have created "pop-up killer" applications designed to automatically close pop-ups or prevent them from opening. To try one of these killer apps designed to squelch these little windows, search for "pop-up killer" on http://download.com.

CREATING A PRESET WINDOW SIZE

16.1 (CP 23)

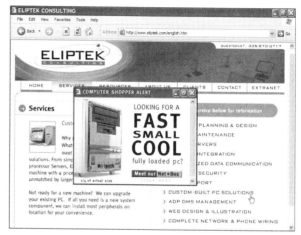

16.2 (CP 24)

B efore you can launch a pop-up window from a page, you must create a separate page that houses the pop-up contents. This step requires planning ahead; first you need to determine what size you want your pop-up to be, then create the graphics and content that go in the pop-up window, and then create the code on a Web page that spawns the pop-up. You generally want to create pop-ups to appear in front of regular, full-sized HTML pages.

If you use the traditional HTML link techniques (such as TARGET="_BLANK") to launch pop-ups, you'll wind up with an odd size such as the one shown in **Figure 16.1 (CP 23)**. This happens because the browser opens at the last size that it was minimized to and closed. In some cases, the browser may even open at a size too small to display the intended content. Note that this also causes the menu bar, URL address, and status bar to appear. You can put all of this to rest with a behavior that manipulates these browser properties on the fly. **Figure 16.2 (CP 24)** shows a correctly sized pop-up window promoting Eliptek Consulting's latest custom computer creations.

STEP 1: PREPARE YOUR POP-UP PAGE

- Create your pop-up Web page and save the document. To use my page, open the file 16_2-popup.htm from the CD.
- Choose **View ➤ Rulers ➤ Show (Ctrl+Alt+R)** to display the rulers along the sides of your document. Take note of the length and width of your pop-up.

STEP 2: PREPARE YOUR POP-UP LAUNCHER

- Create a page to summon the pop-up. For the purpose of this example, the page needs only a BODY tag, so that even the blank default Dreamweaver page is fine. Save your page to continue.

STEP 3: SET THE LINK TO OPEN THE POP-UP

You have many ways to summon pop-up windows. One of the most popular methods is to load the pop-up automatically as soon as the page begins to load. You do this by adding a JavaScript behavior to the BODY tag of the document with the OnLoad property. If you want to launch a pop-up by using a link instead, follow these steps, substituting the BODY tag with the A tag and OnLoad with OnClick.

- Scroll to the top of your launcher page. Click the <body> tag in the Tag inspector to select it.

> **NOTE**
>
> You can find this pop-up page in the Technique 16 folder on the CD-ROM. The filename is 16_2-launcher.htm, and its graphics are in the same folder's images directory.

- With the BODY tag selected, choose **Window ➤ Behaviors (Shift+F3)** to expand the Behaviors panel. Click the **Plus Sign (+)** button and choose **Open Browser Window** from the expanded menu. The Open Browser Window dialog box appears (see **Figure 16.3**).

The Open Browser behavior enables you to set various properties of the pop-up window. Aside from specifying the window size, you can disable the browser navigational menus and even turn off scrollbars if they don't suit your content.

- In the Open Browser Window dialog box, enter the name of the pop-up. Set the size (which you noted in Step 1) and other specifications of your pop-up window, and enter a Window Name. Click **OK** to complete the behavior.

Save your document and test your page. As soon as the launcher page is opened, the pop-up appears in the size you designated, as shown in **Figure 16.4**.

> **TIP**
>
> Because pop-up windows appear in the middle of the screen, the viewer usually sees the page title before the pop-up content loads. Putting a title in at this time is a good idea, or at least remove Dreamweaver's default "untitled page" title. Save your changes.

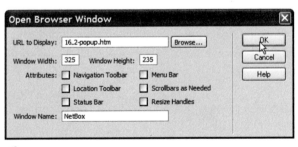

16.3

16.4

CREATING A "GALLERY WALL" USING MULTIPLE POP-UP WINDOWS

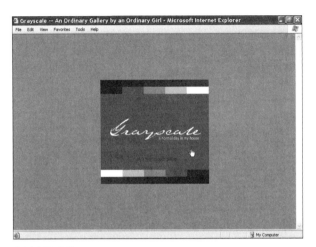

17.1 (CP 25)

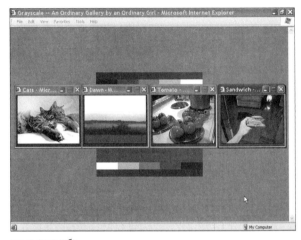

17.2 (CP 26)

One of the coolest things I've ever seen done with pop-up windows is a "gallery wall" (or in context, a gallery *screen*). If you're an artist, this is an ideal way to showcase your work online. **Figure 17.1** (**CP 25**) shows the pop-up window, and **Figure 17.2** (**CP 26**) shows the gallery wall created when the user clicks the pop-up.

STEP 1: INSERT THE OPEN BROWSER WINDOW BEHAVIOR

- Choose **File ➢ Open** and browse to find Technique17.htm.
- Click the Grayscale image in the center of the page to select it.
- With the image selected, click the **Behaviors** tab in the Design panel.
- Click the **Plus Sign** (+) button and choose **Open Browser Window** from the menu.

■ In the Behaviors panel, make sure that the event is listed as (onClick). If it isn't, click the black down arrow and choose (**onClick**) from the menu, as shown in **Figure 17.3**.

■ In the Open Browser Window dialog box, browse for the file called window1.htm. In the dialog box, enter a width and height for your new window. I entered **190** and **145** because the images are each 180 by 185, and I want the window to have a 10-pixel area around the image. Leave all the check boxes unchecked (unless you prefer that any of these window elements are visible). Enter an identifying name, such as gal1, for the window name. See **Figure 17.4**.

17.3

■ With the Grayscale image still selected, repeat this step for the three remaining gallery pages (window2.htm, window3.htm, and window4.htm).

STEP 2: SPECIFY THE POSITION OF EACH WINDOW

For this step, you need to work in Code View to edit the JavaScript created by the Open Browser Window behavior. The position of the windows is up to you. In this technique, I am placing all four windows in a horizontal row, 200 pixels from the top of the screen.

> **NOTE**
>
> You can enter only absolute, or pixel, positions using Dreamweaver's Open Browser Window behavior. The downside of this behavior is that some browsers position the gallery based on the monitor window and not the browser window, causing some interesting — and probably undesired — effects. With a little CSS and DHTML knowledge however, you can specify relative positioning for each gallery window, minimizing undesired positioning. You can learn more about CSS by selecting O'Reilly CSS Reference in Dreamweaver's Reference panel.

■ In Code View, locate the link tag that launches the gallery windows. The piece of code for which you are looking looks something like this, if you have Word Wrap turned on (**View ➢ CodeView Options ➢ Word Wrap**):

```
<a href="#" onClick="MM_openBrWindow
('window1.htm','gal1','width=190,
height=145');
MM_openBrWindow('window2.htm','gal2'
,'width=190,height=145');
```

```
MM_openBrWindow('window3.htm','gal3',
'width=190,height=145');
MM_openBrWindow('window4.htm','gal4',
'width=190,height=145')">
<img src="images/title.gif"
width="300" height="200" border="0">
</a>
```

■ Insert the Top and Left positions for each of the four gallery windows. Here is the code with the Top and Left positions included:

17.4

```
<a href="#" onClick="MM_openBrWindow
('window1.htm','gal1','width=190,
height=145,top=200,left=5');
MM_openBrWindow('window2.htm',
'gal2','width=190,height=145,
top=200,left=200');
MM_openBrWindow('window3.htm',
'gal3','width=190,height=145,
top=200,left=400');
MM_openBrWindow('window4.htm',
'gal4','width=190,height=145,
top=200,left=600')">
<img src="images/title.gif" width=
"300" height="200" border="0">
</a>
```

■ Click **File ➤ Save**.

STEP 3: TEST THE MODIFIED BEHAVIOR IN YOUR BROWSER

■ Press the **F12** key on your keyboard to open your launch page in a browser window. You can view a finished version of this technique by

opening the file called Technique17_finished.htm in the Technique 17 folder on the CD.

■ As soon as the page is open in the browser, click the Grayscale image to launch the gallery. See **Figures 17.5** and **17.6**.

17.5

17.6

18

CREATING TOOL TIPS WITH ONBLUR AND ONFOCUS EVENTS

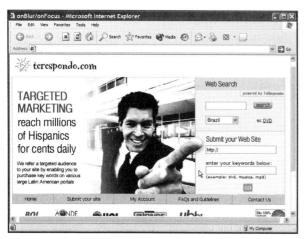

18.1 (CP 27)

18.2 (CP 28)

By using layers and JavaScript behaviors, you can create tool tip windows that display useful information about text fields without cluttering your form. Even with JavaScript form validation techniques, preventing human error is hard when the person doesn't understand what to input. Crowding HTML forms with supplemental instructions is easy, but many people turn away from filling out forms that appear too long and daunting. This technique shows you how to display tool tips next to input boxes that disappear when they are not in use, as shown in **Figures 18.1 (CP 27)** and **18.2 (CP 28)**. Tool tips enable you to help your visitors better understand what you want them to fill out on your forms without scaring them away with unnecessarily long or cluttered form pages.

STEP 1: CREATE A TEXT FIELD

Input fields can't do much without a Form tag.

- Choose **Insert ➣ Form Objects ➣ Text Field** to insert a form field into your document. Dreamweaver asks you if you would like a Form tag added. Click **OK**.
- A red dotted line appears around your text field, as shown in **Figure 18.3**. This indicates that your text field is nested inside a Form tag.

STEP 2: INSERT THE TOOL TIP

Your tool tip resides inside of a layer. Draw your layer near your text field so that the user immediately understands its relevance when it pops up.

- Choose **Insert ➣ Layer**.
- Position the layer near your text field by dragging the layer's handle. The handle is the small square within a square at the top left of the layer indicator. To resize the layer, drag the solid black dots that appear on the sides and corners of the layer when it is selected.

WARNING

This technique is intended for a current browser audience. Older browsers, such as Internet Explorer 3, may produce JavaScript errors when displaying layers. You can use the Dreamweaver MX Browser Check behaviors to design contingency pages.

- Insert your tool tip graphics, or simply type your tool tip into the layer. Set the layer's background color for contrast by using the Property inspector. In this technique, a graphic has been inserted inside the layer.
- With your layer selected, set its Vis (visibility) property to **Hidden** in the menu found on the Property inspector.

Now that the tool tip layer is hidden, you need to assign a behavior that makes it visible when it is needed.

STEP 3: THE ONFOCUS EVENT SHOWS THE TOOL TIP

You need to assign two behaviors for each text field. The first behavior is to show the layer with `OnFocus`, which is triggered when the cursor is clicked inside the text box. To hide the layer as soon as the mouse exits the text field, you'll use the `OnBlur` behavior.

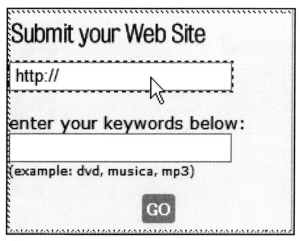

18.3

■ Click to select your text field.

■ Choose **Window** ➢ **Behaviors (Shift+F3)** to display the Behaviors panel. Click the **Plus Sign (+)** button and choose **Show/Hide Layers**. The Show/Hide Layers dialog box appears.

■ Choose your layer and click the **Show** button. The word (show) appears in parentheses next to your layer on the menu. Click **OK** to close the dialog box.

■ An `OnBlur` event appears in the Behaviors panel. Choose the behavior. Click and hold the **event arrow** to reveal more options. Choose **onFocus** (see **Figure 18.4**).

STEP 4: ONBLUR HIDES THE LAYER WHEN INACTIVE

■ Click to select your text field.

■ Click the **Plus Sign (+)** button and choose **Show/Hide Layers** again from the Behaviors panel. The Show/Hide Layers dialog box appears.

■ Choose your layer and click the **Hide** button. The word (hide) appears in parentheses next to your layer on the menu. Click **OK** to close the dialog box.

■ An `OnBlur` event appears in your Behavior panel.

TIP

The easiest and fastest way to create a tool tip is to set a contrasting background color to a layer and type text into it. You can also add images or multimedia files, such as Flash. GIF files are especially effective because of their transparency properties. As shown in Figure 18.2 (CP 28), the tool tip has rounded edges and a protruding pointer.

18.4

This completes the technique. To test it in your Web browser, press **F12**. Click inside the text field you created to display the layer tool tip, and then click somewhere else to hide it. See **Figure 18.5**.

REMINDER

If normal text tool tips are too dull for your tastes, you can create your own designs by using imaging software, such as Fireworks or Photoshop. You can find the tool tip graphic used in this technique in the folder called Technique 18 on the CD-ROM.

TIP

For a creative multimedia effect, use your microphone to create audio tool tips. Save the audio as WAV files individually, and follow the steps in this technique by using the Play Sound behavior in the place of the Show/Hide Layer behavior — or create two `onFocus` events to do both. Keep in mind the file size of your WAVs so that they load quickly when they are referenced, or you may experience a delayed response.

18.5

FLOATING POP-UPS WITHOUT WINDOWS

19.1 (CP 29)   19.2 (CP 30)

T he floating layer pop-up is the latest craze in online advertising. The floating pop-up is essentially a DHTML layer with various supporting JavaScript behaviors associated to it. This is how it frees itself from needing its own window in which to appear. Unlike JavaScript pop-ups, which launch separate browser windows, this technique embeds the pop-up within the Web page. You have more control over floating pop-ups — such as where to position the close button. Now that the majority of America Online users have browsers that support DHTML, large portals, such as Yahoo! and AOL, have begun allowing such campaigns to run in their networks. In the following steps, you create a floating pop-up that opens at a designated time after the page loads and automatically closes itself after a few seconds.

Look ma, no borders! As shown in **Figure 19.2 (CP 30)**, you can use transparency properties in your artwork to give the pop-up any shape you like.

STEP 1: POPULATE THE FLOATING POP-UP

■ Open the Web page where you'd like the floating pop-up to appear. Click **Insert ➢ Layer** to insert a blank DHTML layer.

■ Click inside the layer and insert your graphics, texts, or rich media files.

STEP 2: DESIGNATE THE LAUNCH BEHAVIOR

Similar to traditional pop-ups, floating pop-ups rely on JavaScript actions to spawn them. In Technique 16, you used the OnLoad command to launch a browser window when the page loads. With floating pop-ups, you can designate more levels of control because there are a variety of possibilities when working with layers. You can use the timeline feature in Dreamweaver to set a timer for the pop-up. In the following steps, you create a pop-up that opens after ten seconds, closes itself automatically after ten seconds, and gives the user the option of closing it early.

■ Choose **Windows ➢ Others ➢ Layers (F2)** to reveal the Layers panel. Click the layer that you just created. Optionally, you can give the layer a name in this panel. The Layers panel is a member

---

TIP

If your entire pop-up content is a GIF89 file, you can set a matte or mask transparency in your imaging program to give the pop-up a unique shape. You can do the same with a Flash movie by creating a new parameter for it by using the Parameters Editor within the Property inspector. Enter the Window Mode parameter (**WMODE**) and enter the value as **Transparent**.

---

of the Advanced Layout panel group. If this group is already open, just click the Layers tab to open the Layers panel.

■ Choose **Windows ➢ Others ➢ Timelines (Alt+F9)** to reveal the Timelines panel options menu. With your layer selected, click the **Timelines** panel options menu and choose **Add Object** (see **Figure 19.3**). Your layer appears with two keyframes on the timelines (see **Figure 19.4**). Check the **Autoplay** check box. This adds an OnLoad JavaScript to your BODY tag, which follows whatever you specify in the timeline when the page loads.

■ Click the first **keyframe**. Click the space next to the layer name in the visibility icon to reveal the eye icon. Click again to reveal the closed eye icon. Your layer is now invisible.

■ Click the second **keyframe**. Drag it to the desired frame when you'd like the pop-up to appear. Because the layer was set to visible by default in this keyframe, you need not set the visibility mode for it. This concludes the launch sequence of the pop-up.

You have two common ways to hide floating pop-ups. You can set a scheduled hide action by using the timeline, and/or you can create a hot spot in the ad where the visibility of the layer is set to hide. The next few steps illustrate how to do both.

STEP 3: SCHEDULE A FLOATING POP-UP TO HIDE

You want this pop-up to show for only ten seconds, so you can determine the frame number by multiplying the number of seconds by the frame rate (150), and then adding the amount of frames that already exist in the sequence (15).

■ Scroll to the desired frame in the Timelines panel. For a pause of ten seconds, select frame 165.

19.3

■ With your desired frame selected, click the **Timelines** button and choose **Add a Keyframe**.

■ Click your layer in the Layers panel. Click the visibility column until your layer is set to hide. This concludes the automated hide procedure. Save and press **F12** to test in your browser.

STEP 4: ADD A CLOSE BUTTON BEHAVIOR

One of the great features about floating pop-ups is that you can choose whether to have a close button. If

NOTE

You can find the completed scheduler in the folder called Technique 19 on the CD-ROM. The filename is 19-step2.htm.

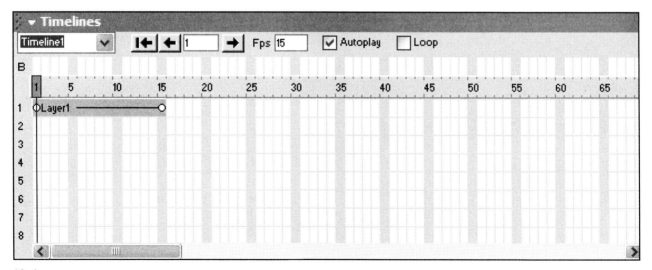

19.4

you choose to have one, you can design it to look like anything and place it anywhere. Even if users want to close the pop-up, their eyes are going to hunt all over the ad looking for that button.

■ Insert some text or a button into your layer to set up for the behavior. If your original design has a close button drawn in like the one shown in **Figure 19.5**, you can draw an image map.

■ In the Behaviors panel, click the **Plus Sign** (+) button and choose **Show/Hide Layers** with your link, button, or image map selected.

■ In the Show-Hide Layers dialog box, click your layer and click the **Hide** button (see **Figure 19.6**). Click **OK** to close the dialog box. Save and test in your browser. See **Figure 19.7**.

19.5

19.6

Welcome to the

In this issue you

How to Exp

How to Create a Flash Menu in Dreamweaver

How to Create a Template Driven Web Site

In the DWMX Extensions Spotlight: InstaGraphics Extension

component, we can install most peripherals on location for your convenience.

> WEB DESIGN & ILLUSTRATION

> COMPLETE NETWORK & PHONE WIRING

19.7

DELIVERING A MESSAGE QUIETLY WITH POP-UNDER WINDOWS

20.1 (CP 31)

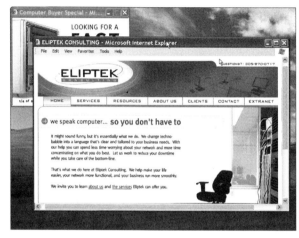

20.2 (CP 32)

Pop-under windows, shown in **Figure 20.2 (CP 32)**, are a great way to send messages to visitors without interfering with their Web browsing. Users generally do not see pop-under windows until after they close their main browser window.

You create a pop-under window in the same way that you create a pop-up window. The only difference is that an additional JavaScript event is required that prevents the pop-up from coming into the foreground. Pop-under windows are most widely used by sites that want to deliver advertisements from other companies, but do not want these ads to be in the foreground while the user browses their site.

STEP 1: CREATE THE POP-UNDER WINDOW FILE

■ Follow the steps in Technique 16 to create a pop-up window and a launcher.

STEP 2: ADD THE CUSTOM SCRIPT

The little known fact about pop-unders is that they don't actually pop-under. The launcher page calls up the pop-up window event, but then another event immediately forces itself as the "focus," which causes the pop-up to get moved behind the parent window. The pop-up resides immediately behind the launcher where it cannot be seen, thereby becoming a pop-under.

To turn your pop-up window (See **Figure 20.3**) into a pop-under window, follow these steps:

- Open the page where you created the pop-up launcher.
- Click the `<body>` tag in the Tag inspector to select it.
- Click the **Plus Sign** (+) button in the Behaviors panel and choose **Call JavaScript**.
- In the Call JavaScript dialog box, enter the following code: **window.focus()**.
- Click **OK** (see **Figure 20.4**).

The pop-under is now complete. Save and navigate to your folder to open the file manually to preview it in a browser.

NOTE

Close all of your browser windows before testing your work. Previewing this technique by using the Dreamweaver F12 key command may not be effective because it launches a new browser window when you press F12. In some cases, both windows may open minimized, depending on your configuration.

20.4

TIP

Users generally don't notice pop-under windows until they close their main browser window. You can use this opportunity to load high bandwidth content that you would not normally ask people to wait for or to deliver messages that you want them to see after they are done looking at a site.

20.3

INVITING THEM BACK TO YOUR SITE WITH AN EXIT POP-UP WINDOW

21.1

21.2

Exit pop-up windows enable you to make the best of outgoing site traffic. By using JavaScript behaviors, you can launch a pop-up window the very second users leave your Web site or close their Web browser, as shown in **Figure 21.2**. There are many useful applications for pop-up windows on exit. For example, if your site offers e-commerce, you can pop-up a last chance bargain to invite them back to shop on your site.

The same principles of creating a pop-up window from the previous techniques apply. The only difference in steps is the OnUnload event, which triggers as soon as the browser closes.

STEP 1: CREATE THE POP-UP WINDOW FILE

■ Follow the steps in Technique 16 to create a standard pop-up. In Technique 16, you create two Web pages, one for the pop-up and one for the launcher.

STEP 2: MODIFY THE LAUNCHER EVENT

■ Open the page where you created the pop-up launcher.
■ Click the `<body>` tag in the Tag inspector to select it.
■ You see the `OnLoad` event assigned to the pop-up behavior. Click to select the **OnUnload** event (see **Figure 21.3**).
■ Save and preview your work by pressing **F12**.
■ Allow the page to load completely, and then close your browser to view the result. See **Figure 21.4**.

TIP

When finalizing your pop-up window, always consider the `TARGET` of the links that you create. If you launch a pop-up that does not allow scrolling or resizing, and your links all use the default target, the linked pages will be constrained in that tiny box. Most designers use `_blank` as their `TARGET`, which opens a full sized browser window.

NOTE

In addition to the browser being closed, the `OnUnload` event also goes off when the browser is refreshed.

NOTE

If the user closes the page before your browser has a chance to interpret the pop-up code, your pop-up window will not appear. Similarly, a "pop-up killer" application also prevents pop-up windows from working.

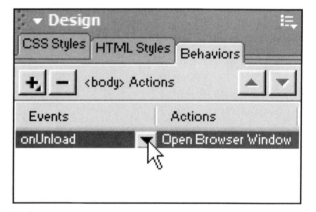

21.3

21.4

CHAPTER 5

ADVANCED PAGE DESIGN TECHNIQUES

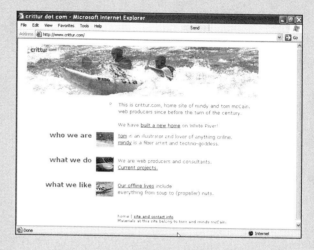

Designers who are used to working in print get frustrated very quickly when they start working on the Web. Okay, truth be told, most people who have good design sense get frustrated at least once in a while by the limited design control you have when creating HTML pages. But before you get too annoyed with all of the limitations, spend some time exploring the techniques in this chapter, which are designed to help you take advantage of some of Dreamweaver's best design features. You should also know that as the Web has matured, HTML has evolved to include more and more cool features, such as floating layers, covered in Technique 25 at the end of this chapter.

For the most part, when you want to create anything but the simplest design on a Web page, you should use the HTML feature known as *tables*. Tables on a Web page are used for far more than organizing numerical data. When used effectively, they provide one of the best ways to align elements on a page and provide real design control.

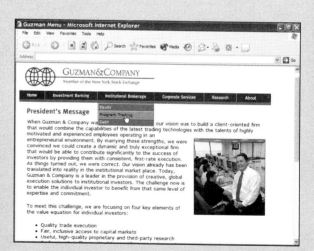

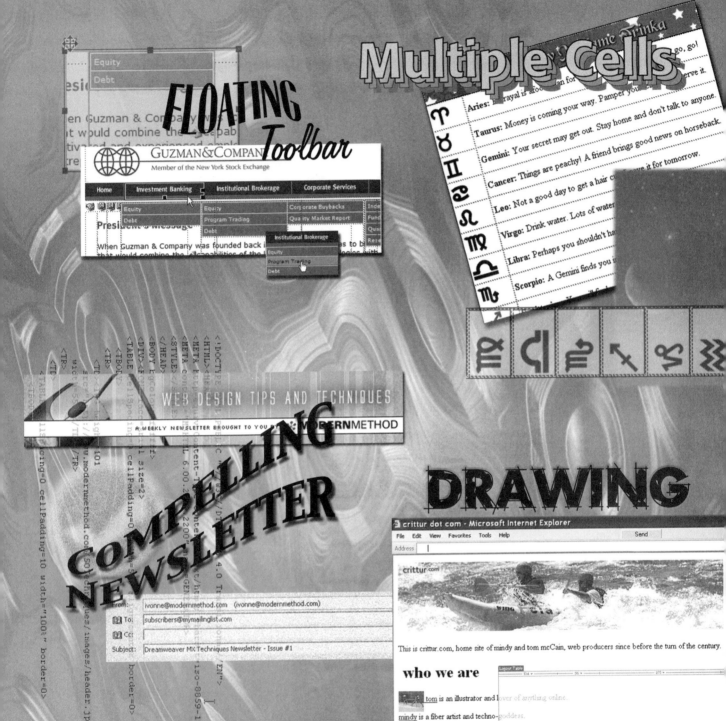

"DRAWING" TABLES WITH LAYOUT FEATURES

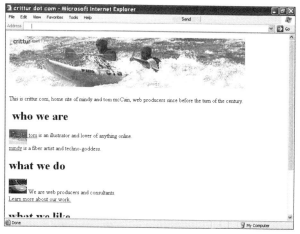

22.1 (CP 33)

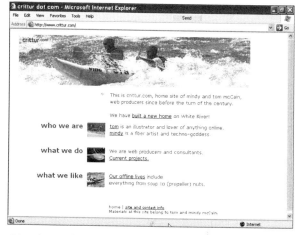

22.2 (CP 34)

Tables are by far one of the most important design elements used on the Web, but they are a little complicated to create, especially if you're working on a really complex page layout. That's why the Dreamweaver Table Layout feature is so cool. With it, you can "draw" a table on a page, creating cells wherever you want in a way that is much more intuitive than splitting and merging cells. You can achieve the alignment you want with tables, as shown in **Figure 22.2 (CP 34)**. If you couldn't use tables, you'd have limited design control over a page, as shown in **Figure 22.1 (CP 33)**.

STEP 1: DRAW A TABLE

The easiest way to work with tables in Dreamweaver is to switch to Layout View and use the special Layout Cell and Layout Table tools. With these tools, which are available only in Layout View, Dreamweaver makes it possible to place your cursor anywhere on the screen and "draw" a table cell by clicking and dragging. That's right, you can just place your cursor anywhere on the page, create a cell any size you want, and then insert any content you want: images, text, multimedia files, and so forth.

Dreamweaver makes it possible to draw a cell wherever you want it by automatically generating the rest of the table and the necessary cells around your new cell. See **Figure 22.3** to see what this looks like in action. I created the outline of the table in Layout View (you find details in the steps below). As soon as the outline of the table was created, I simply drew in the two cells that appear in white by clicking and dragging them into place. The outline of the newest cell is in black because I was in the process of drawing it in when I took the screen shot. The gray cells appeared automatically around my cells to keep the spacing the way I wanted. Dreamweaver also uses transparent images in table cells to provide exact positioning.

Using transparent images is an old trick in Web design that takes advantage of the fact that you can change the size of an image to anything you want in

> **TIP**
>
> The first time you choose Layout View, you find a message with a brief description of how to use the Layout Table and Layout Cell buttons. You may find this a handy reminder and want to keep it, but if you get tired of it, check "Don't show me this message again" to prevent seeing it in the future. Either way, click **OK** to close it.

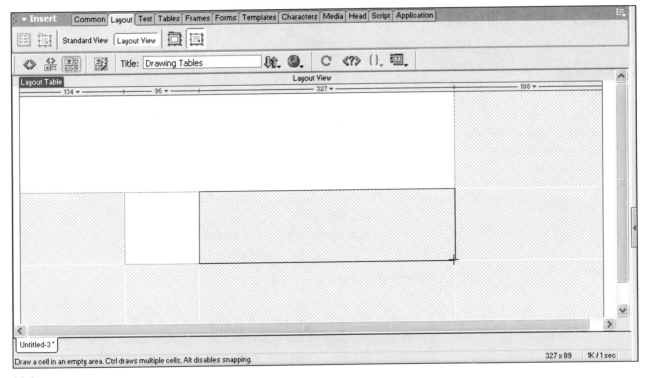

22.3

the HTML code. For example, you can stretch a small image into a larger one or shrink a large image to a smaller one. In general, you don't want to do this because it can distort the image, but if you place a transparent, and therefore invisible, image on a page and then adjust the size, you can use it to control spacing. You simply adjust the transparent image to exactly fill the space you want to control, and then use the image to position other elements precisely on the page. Dreamweaver automatically does this for you, in the background when you use Layout View to create a table.

Of course, you can still create tables the old-fashioned way in Standard View. You can easily switch between the two modes, which is important because you have more editing controls in Standard View. You're probably already used to working in Standard View in Dreamweaver because that's the default for working on documents. Layout View provides a special view mode designed to assist in the constructing and editing of tables, and it's unique to Dreamweaver.

To create a table in Layout View with a long cell across the top and two smaller cells below it (such as the table shown in Figure 22.2 (CP 34)), create a new HTML page and follow these steps:

- Switch to Layout View by clicking the **Layout** tab in the Insert bar and then clicking the **Layout View** button. You can also switch to Layout View by choosing **View ➤ Table View ➤ Layout View**, but I find the Layout tab in the Insert bar is more convenient.

- Click the **Draw Layout Table** button, and then click and drag to create the outline of the table on your Web page. (In Figure 22.3, you can see where I drew the table outline because it provides the outside frame of the table area.) You can always resize the table area by clicking and dragging any of the borders or by changing the values in the width and height text boxes in the Property inspector.
- Click the **Draw Layout Cell** button, and you see that the cursor changes to a crosshair when you move the mouse over the document area. The crosshair indicates you can draw a table cell.
- Click the mouse on the document, and while holding down the mouse button, drag to draw a rectangular shape across the top of the page for your first table cell. In Figure 22.3, I'm adding a new cell in the middle of the table to demonstrate how easy it is to "draw" a new cell anywhere on the page.
- The cell is drawn and its surrounding table structure is automatically generated. A grid representing the table structure appears with the current cell shown in white.
- Below the cell you just drew, draw a small, square shape such as the cell shown in Figure 22.3. Each time you draw a new cell, you have to click the **Draw Layout Cell** button again and then click and drag on the page where you want the cell.
- You can continue to draw cells by clicking the **Draw Layout Cell** button and then clicking and dragging on the page.

TIP

As you draw, notice that the cell "snaps" into place along the guidelines in the table grid. Use the grid as a guide in lining up your cells.

REMINDER

You can add any content into a table cell that you can add anywhere else on a page, including images, text, and multimedia files.

Depending on where you started drawing your table cells, Dreamweaver may create table cells around the cells you created to maintain their position on the page. For example, in the table shown in Figure 22.3, although I only created three new cells, Dreamweaver has filled in the gaps by automatically creating more cells, so that there are actually 10 cells in this final table.

In Standard View a table defaults to the top-left corner of a page, so the first cells in the table are close to the top-left margin. However, using Layout View, you can draw cells wherever you want them on a page, and Dreamweaver automatically generates the other cells that are needed to keep the positioning you created in Layout View. Using tables is one of the easiest ways to place elements exactly where you want them on a page. Empty cells that Dreamweaver creates to fill space in a table merely act as *spacer cells* and don't show up in the browser, giving the illusion that various page elements are positioned independently on any part of the page.

STEP 2: EDIT TABLES IN LAYOUT VIEW

One of the really wonderful features about working with tables in Layout View is that you can use the layout grid to edit, move, and resize any of the rows, columns, and cells in the table. This allows you to use the grid as a design guide for creating any kind of layout you want. Normally, the only way to create complicated layouts in HTML is by meticulously building complex tables and carefully splitting and merging cells manually. Using Layout View, you can simply draw cells wherever you want them and create asymmetric tables quickly and easily for complex design work.

- To edit a table cell in Layout View, simply click any border and drag it to the desired size, as shown in **Figure 22.4**.
- To access other table editing features, such as **Border Color** and **Background Image**, switch to Standard View by clicking the **Standard View** button in the Insert bar or choosing **View ➢ Table View ➢ Standard View**.

For the final Web site, see **Figure 22.5**.

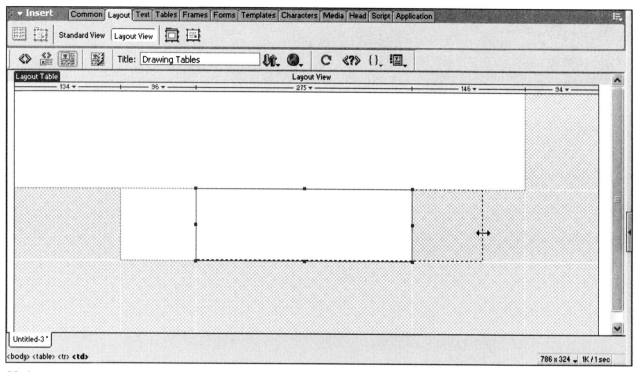

22.4

This is crittur.com, home site of mindy and tom mcCain, web producers since before the turn of the century.

We have built a new home on White River!

who we are tom is an illustrator and lover of anything online. mindy is a fiber artist and techno-goddess.

what we do We are web producers and consultants. Current projects.

what we like Our offline lives include everything from soup to (propeller) nuts.

home | site and contact info
Materials at this site belong to tom and mindy mcCain.

22.5

Technique 1:
Using Tracing Images to Re-create Designs

Dreamweaver's unique Tracing Image feature enables you to use an image to guide your design work.

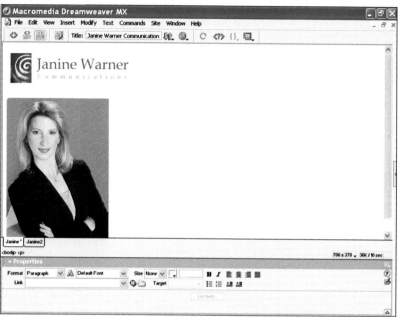

CP 1

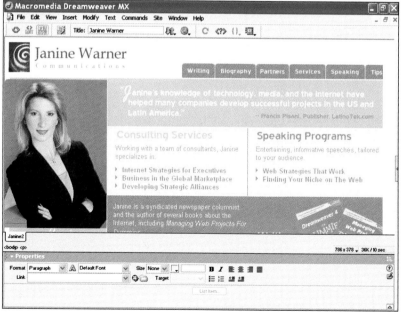

CP 2

Technique 2:
Creating Rollovers for Interactivity

Adding a simple rollover effect to a button tells a Web site user that this item can be clicked.

CP 3

CP 4

Technique 3:
Setting Links in an Image Map

Dreamweaver makes it easy to create image hot spots that link to different URLs.

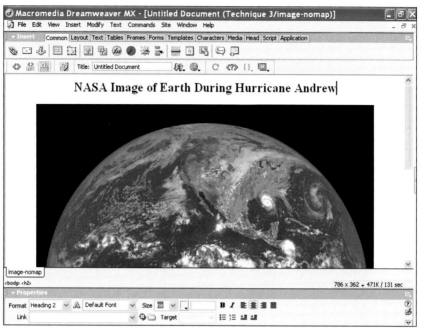

CP 5

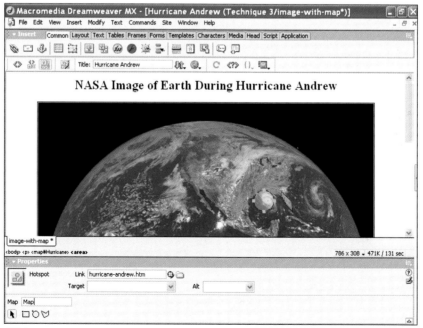

CP 6

Technique 4:

Exporting a Layout from Fireworks into Dreamweaver

You can build your entire Web page layout in Fireworks and then, using the slice tool and export feature, let Fireworks build the HTML page for you. You can then open the new HTML page in Dreamweaver to continue your work.

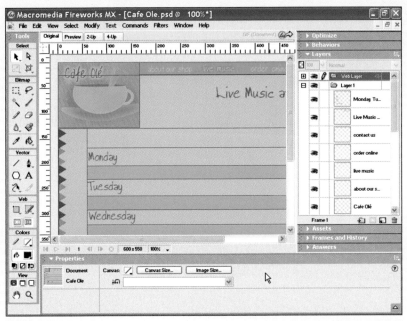

CP 7

CP 8

Technique 6:
Finding and Fixing Broken Links Automatically

Dreamweaver's Link checking features quickly locate and list all broken links. You can then have Dreamweaver fix broken links automatically.

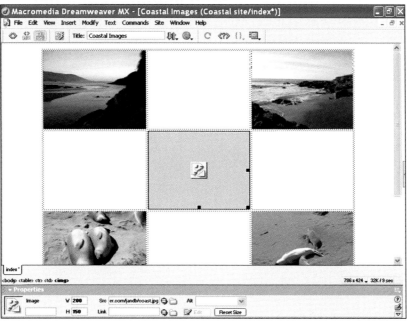

CP 9

CP 10

Technique 7:
Creating a Template-Based Web Site

Dreamweaver's Template feature takes the toil out of creating multiple pages that share the same format.

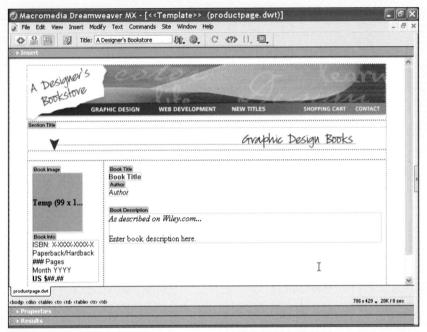

CP 11

CP 12

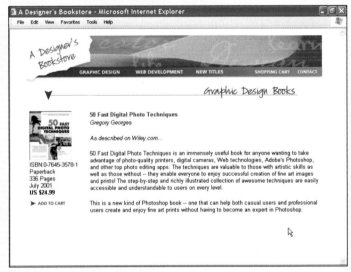

CP 13

Technique 9:

Accessing URLs, Colors, and Images Assets

Dreamweaver's Assets panel group automatically stores every image, color, link, and multimedia file you used in your site. This makes it easy to find various elements when you want to add them to more pages.

CP 14

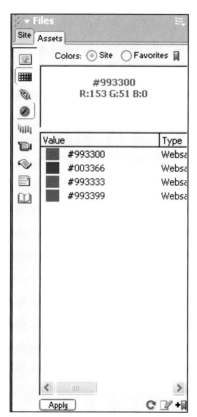

CP 15

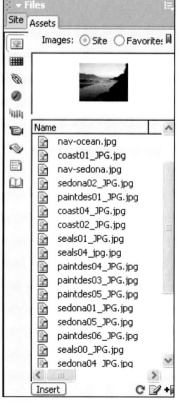

CP 16

Technique 10:
Organizing Files and Folders without Breaking Links

Use the Site panel to add folders, rename elements, and move files around. Dreamweaver automatically adjusts their respective links.

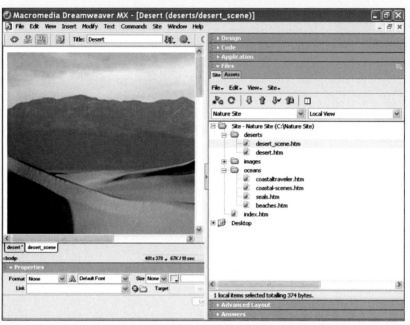

CP 17

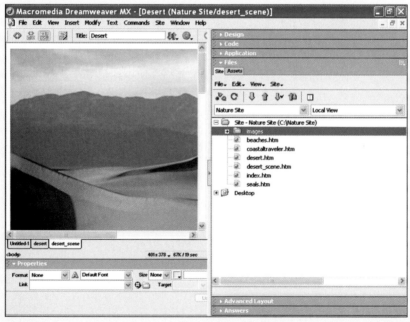

CP 18

Building Rollovers in Fireworks and Exporting Them to Dreamweaver

You can add rollover effects to your layout as you build it in Fireworks. When you open the file in Dreamweaver, click one of the rollover images and notice how the rollover behaviors automatically appear in the Behaviors palette.

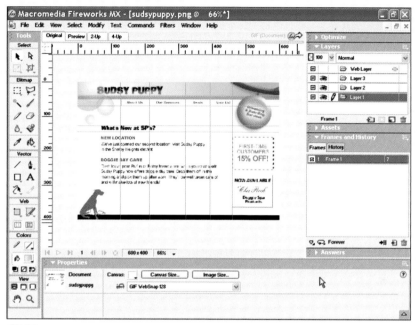

CP 19

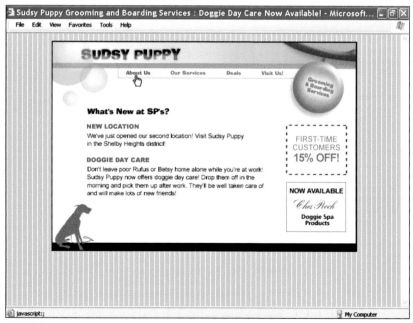

CP 20

Technique 14:
Embedding a Multimedia File

You can add video or other multimedia files to your Web site by embedding them right on your page.

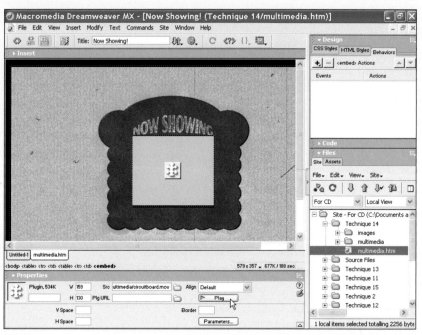

CP 21

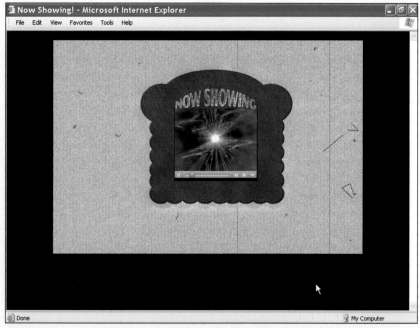

CP 22

Creating a Preset Window Size

Using the traditional HTML link techniques to launch pop-ups can result in oddly sized windows. A preset window size prevents this common problem.

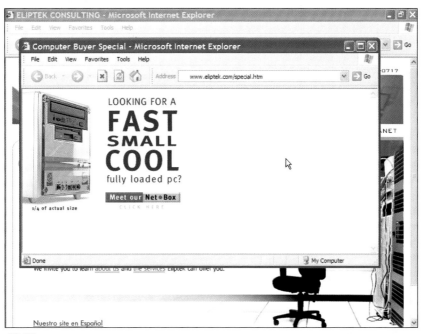

CP 23

CP 24

Technique 17:
Creating a "Gallery Wall" Using Multiple Pop-Up Windows

Show off the best pieces from your portfolio, or photos from your last trip using this easy technique.

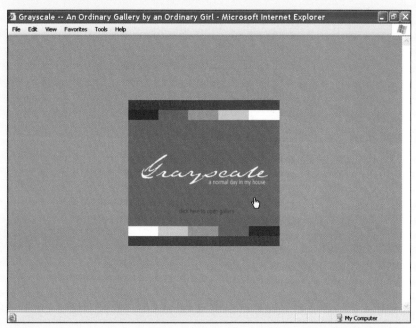

CP 25

CP 26

Creating Tool Tips with OnBlur and OnFocus Events

Breathe new life into your Web forms by moving your static help text into dynamic tool tips.

CP 27

CP 28

Technique 19:
Floating Pop-Ups without Windows

Overlay graphics and text over your Web pages without the use of pop-up windows.

CP 29

CP 30

Technique 20:
Delivering a Message Quietly with Pop-Under Windows

Launch and hide pop-up windows behind the active Web browser with this technique.

CP 31

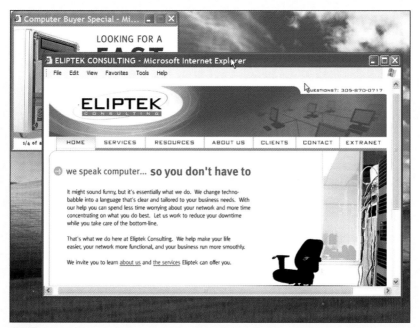

CP 32

"Drawing" Tables with Layout Features

Create complex designs quickly and easily by using Layout View to "draw" tables and cells anywhere on a page.

CP 33

CP 34

Technique 24:
Designing a Compelling HTML E-mail Newsletter

Don't settle for plain old text e-mail anymore: You can make your newsletter or other promotional e-mail come to life with Dreamweaver's great formatting options.

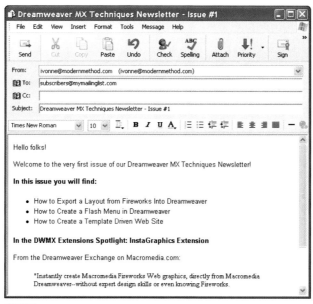

CP 35

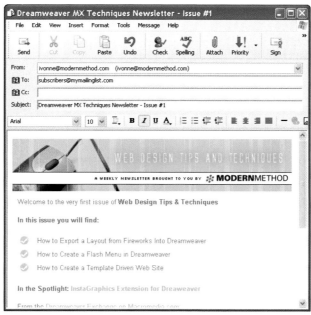

CP 36

Creating a Floating DHTML Toolbar

You can use a floating layer to build a menu that expands dynamically over the body of the page. When the mouse moves away from the menu, the menu disappears automatically.

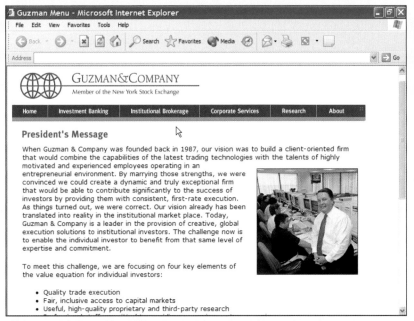

CP 37

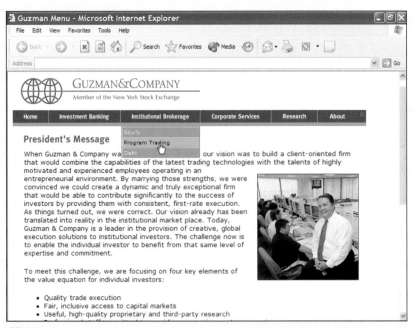

CP 38

Technique 26:
Using Dreamweaver's Accessibility Tools

Dreamweaver's accessibility tools check for accessible development features, such as Alt tags behind images. Alt tags are important to visually impaired Web surfers: Their browsers "read" Web pages to them, describing images with the Alt information.

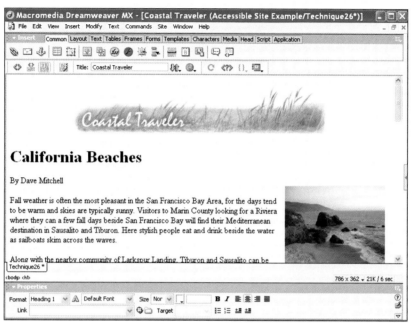

CP 39

CP 40

Providing Multiple Navigation Options

To reach the broadest possible audience, make sure you provide text-based alternatives for navigation. The text links at the bottom of this page match the image rollovers used for navigation at the top of the page.

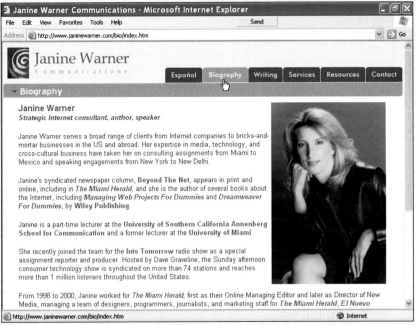

CP 41

CP 42

Technique 30:
"Zooming In" with Rollovers

Combine rollovers and image maps to create a close-up of an area of an image. When you mouse over a certain part of the image map, it appears to zoom to that area of the image.

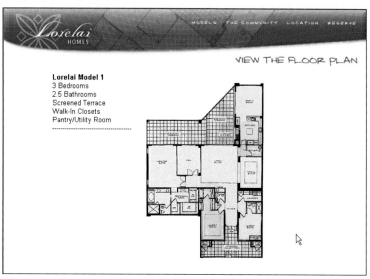

CP 43

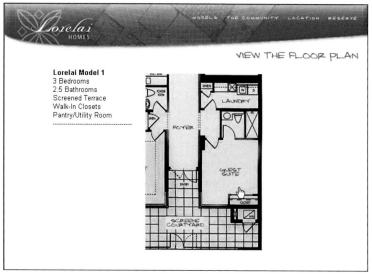

CP 44

Technique 31:
Editing Images from within Dreamweaver

You can set up Dreamweaver to work with Macromedia Fireworks. Then, you can edit images with the push of a button and save changes without ever having to completely leave Dreamweaver.

CP 45

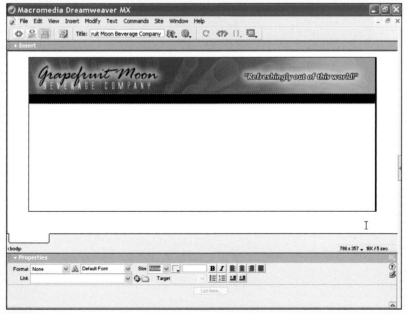

CP 46

Technique 34:

Adding Style to Your Page with a Fixed Tiling Background

A simple change, such as a background, adds style and life to an otherwise bland Web page.

CP 47

CP 48

Technique 35:
Preventing Backgrounds from Tiling and Scrolling

Using CSS, you can force backgrounds to stay in place and prevent them from scrolling no matter how big the user's screen.

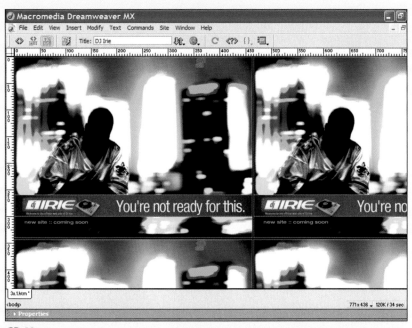

CP 49

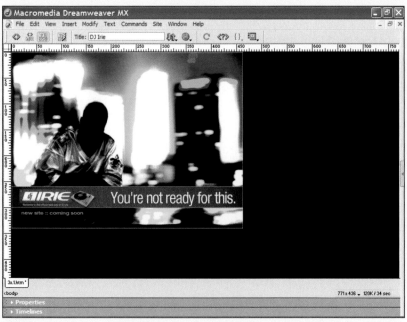

CP 50

Technique 37:
Creating a Library of Common Elements

The Library feature enables you to store a commonly used element, such as a navigation row, and easily add it to any page. Best of all, if you change a Library item, Dreamweaver automatically updates every page containing the Library item.

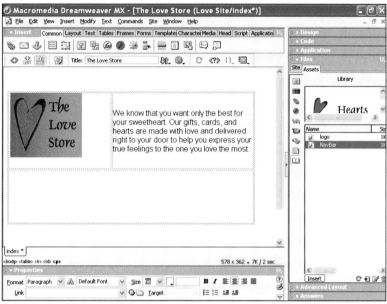

CP 51

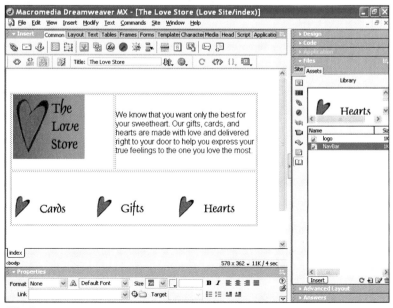

CP 52

Creating Effective Frame Navigation

Dreamweaver makes it easy to create Frames, which you can use to set off navigation elements in one part of a browser window. You can then open their respective links in another part of a browser window.

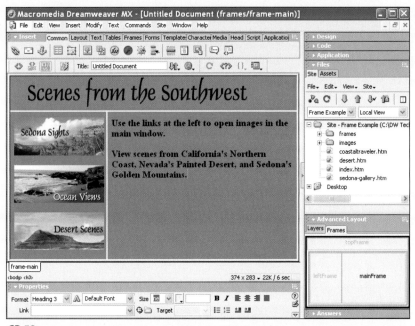

CP 53

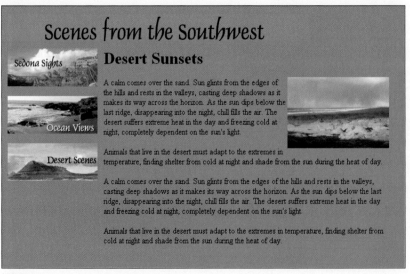

CP 54

Using HTML Styles to Automate Formatting

HTML Styles enable you to alter HTML tags. This helps you format faster and keep page designs more consistent.

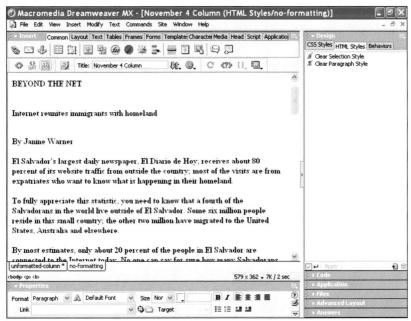

CP 55

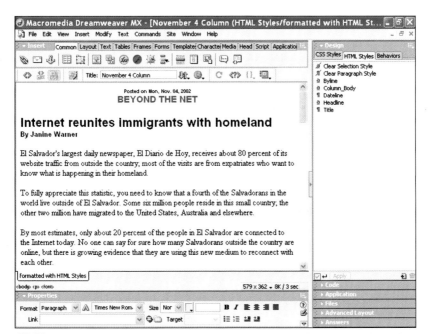

CP 56

Scouring Your Database with an Easy Site Search Feature

With a site search, users can query your database and view matching results through a Web browser. For example, a fantasy football league Web site can use a database search based on zip codes to match local members.

CP 57

CP 58

Showing Off a Product Catalog with a Master/Detail Page Set

You can generate an interactive product catalog using Dreamweaver's database features.

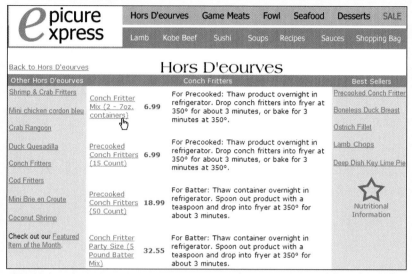

CP 59

CP 60

Technique 46:
Keeping Your Site Looking Fresh with a Random Image Group

Automate dynamically rotating images on your site with this Dreamweaver extension.

CP 61

CP 62

Technique 47:
Accepting Credit Card Payments with PayPal Shopping Cart

This feature enables site visitors purchase goods and services on your site without a merchant account. PayPal Shopping Cart is a hosted secure payment services platform.

CP 63

CP 64

Technique 49:

Preventing Orphaned Frame Content with Framestuffer

Users can open framed pages without their related pages, missing key information, such as navigation elements. This technique shows you how to ensure that framed pages stay together so that your framed pages won't be displayed without their counterparts.

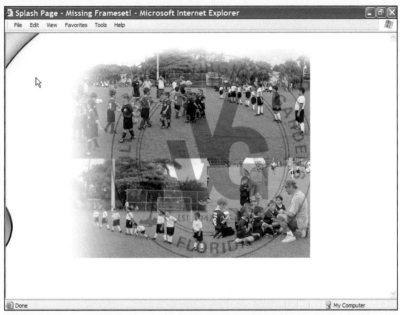

CP 65

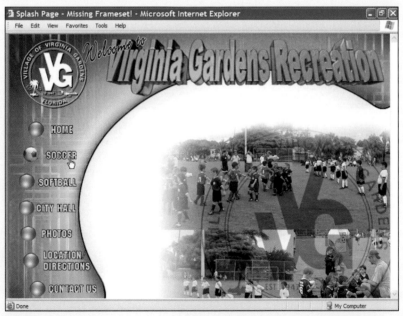

CP 66

FORMATTING MULTIPLE TABLE CELLS

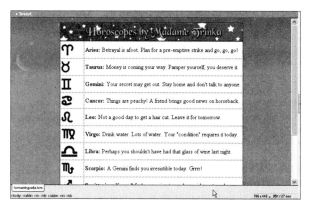

23.1

23.2

I f you have a table with various consecutive cells that require the same formatting, you can quickly format them all at once! I've changed the text alignment and font in **Figure 23.2**.

STEP 1: ALIGN THE CONTENT IN MULTIPLE CELLS

■ Make sure you are in Standard View (**View ➤ Table View ➤ Standard View**). Click inside the top-left column containing the Aries symbol and drag down to select the remaining cells below it.

- With all the cells in the left column selected, click the **Horizontal Alignment** down arrow in the Property inspector. Select an alignment option, as shown in **Figure 23.3**.
  - The symbols now appear center-aligned.

STEP 2: FORMAT THE TEXT IN MULTIPLE CELLS

- Click inside the top-right column that contains the text of the Aries horoscope, and drag down to select the remaining cells below it.
- With all the cells in the right column selected, click the **Font** down arrow in the Property inspector and choose **Arial, Helvetica, sans-serif**.

- Next, click the **Size** down arrow in the Property inspector and choose **2**.
- The text now appears in Arial, size 2.

STEP 3: APPLY A BACKGROUND IMAGE TO MULTIPLE CELLS

- Click inside the top-right column that contains the text of the Aries horoscope and drag down to select the remaining cells below it.
- With all the cells in the right column selected, click the **Browse** button next to the Background Image field in the Property inspector to browse for an image.
- Choose the file named cellbg.gif. Click **OK**.
- The image now appears in every cell in the right column. See **Figure 23.4**.

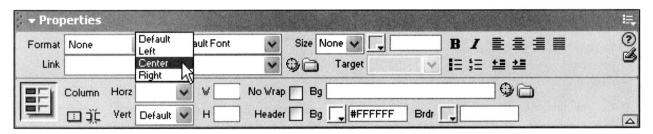

23.3

23.4

DESIGNING A COMPELLING HTML E-MAIL NEWSLETTER

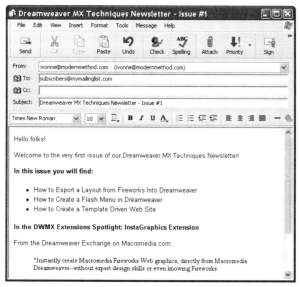

24.1 (CP 35)

24.2 (CP 36)

In this technique, you turn a boring text-based e-mail newsletter into a visually appealing HTML e-mail. **Figures 24.1 (CP 35)** and **24.2 (CP 36)** demonstrate the difference.

These days, we all get so much e-mail that sometimes good messages slip through the cracks. If they don't grab our attention or don't immediately show what they're about, we're likely to press that delete key quickly. Sometimes we even subscribe to e-mail newsletters and then delete them without ever reading them, especially if they appear very long and text-heavy!

A word of warning: Not all e-mail programs can send or receive HTML-formatted e-mails. Also, even if you have an e-mail program that does allow HTML-formatted e-mails, for example at work, your company's firewall may have this option blocked. This technique assumes you will be using Outlook or Outlook Express to send your HTML e-mails.

STEP 1: BUILD YOUR NEWSLETTER IN DREAMWEAVER

In this step, you build your newsletter the way you would build any other HTML page in Dreamweaver. As an alternative, you can work with the sample provided on the CD-ROM.

■ Choose **File ➤ Open** to open the Technique24.htm file (see **Figure 24.3**).
■ Edit this file to suit your needs, adding or removing images and text or changing the layout or color scheme.

STEP 2: UPLOAD IMAGES AND UPDATE IMAGE SOURCE LINKS

In order for images to show up on your HTML e-mail message when a recipient opens it, all images need to be hosted on a Web server.

■ Click the **Expand/Collapse** icon to open the split view Site Panel.
■ Click the **Connect** icon to connect to your Web server.
■ In the Remote Site window, locate the directory in which you want to place your e-mail message image files.

■ In the Local Site window, select the files you want to upload and drag them to the directory in the Remote Site window.

STEP 3: MAKE IMAGE SOURCE PATHS ABSOLUTE

■ On your HTML page, change the image source path to the absolute path on your Web server. For example, the header image source path changes from `images/header.jpg` to `http://www.yourwebsite.com/images/header.jpg`. To make this change, you can select your image in Design View and edit the image Src field in the Property inspector to reflect the change noted above.
■ Make sure that any links to other pages on your server are also absolute. You can make the change by selecting any part of the link in Design View and editing the link field in the Property inspector.

STEP 4A: SEND YOUR HTML E-MAIL FROM OUTLOOK

Now that you prepared your e-mail in Dreamweaver, it's time to send it!

■ In Outlook, open a new e-mail message by choosing **File ➤ New ➤ Mail Message**.

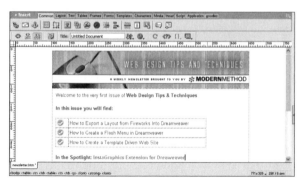

24.3

> **NOTE**
>
> If you use another application to FTP your files to your Web server, please use it as you would normally. It is not necessary to upload your files using Dreamweaver.

- Make sure that the format of the e-mail is HTML. You can check this by choosing **Format** ➤ **HTML** on the menu in the New Message window.
- Place your cursor in the message body area and choose **Insert** ➤ **File**. The Insert File dialog box appears.
- Browse for the Technique24.htm file and click it once to select it.
- Click the down arrow next to the Insert button and choose **Insert as Text** from the menu that appears. The content of Technique24.htm appears in the body of the e-mail message exactly as you created it in Dreamweaver. See **Figure 24.4**.

STEP 4B: SEND YOUR HTML E-MAIL FROM OUTLOOK EXPRESS

Sending your HTML e-mail from Outlook Express is slightly different, though just as quick and easy.

- In Outlook Express, open a new e-mail message by choosing **File** ➤ **New** ➤ **Mail Message**.
- Make sure that the format of the e-mail is Rich Text (HTML). You can check this by choosing **Format** ➤ **Rich Text (HTML)** on the menu in the New Message window.

- Place your cursor in the message body area and choose **Insert** ➤ **Text from File**. The Insert Text File dialog box appears.
- Choose **HTML Files** from the Files of Type menu at the bottom of the dialog box. Then, browse for the Technique24.htm file. Double-click it to insert it into your mail message. The content of Technique24.htm appears in the body of the e-mail message exactly as you created it in Dreamweaver. See **Figure 24.5**.

TIP

Occasionally, some text may lose formatting or may look quirky after the HTML is inserted into the mail message. Usually, you can fix these minor details inside that mail message using the text formatting tools provided in the e-mail program. However, HTML editing capabilities in a mail message window are never as robust as those in Dreamweaver. Using Dreamweaver for major changes to the layout is best.

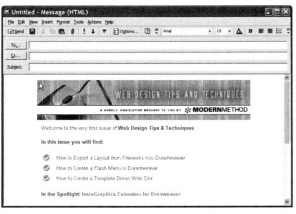

24.4

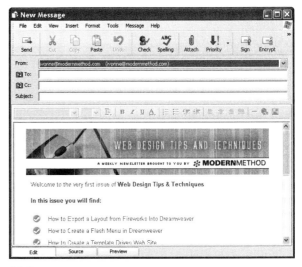

24.5

As previously mentioned, sometimes text may lose formatting, or the layout may look slightly different in the mail message. With Outlook Express you have a bit more flexibility for making changes because you can view and edit the HTML source code of your message. To view your message as pure HTML, choose **View ➢ Source Edit**. Three tabs appear on the bottom of your mail message: Edit, Source, and Preview (see **Figure 24.6**). Click the **Source** tab to

edit the HTML source code, and then click the **Preview** tab to see how your sent message will look. To edit just text, you can work in the **Edit** tab. Keep in mind that editing your e-mail in Outlook Express will *not* save the changes to the original HTML file, Technique24.htm. See **Figure 24.7** for the finished newsletter.

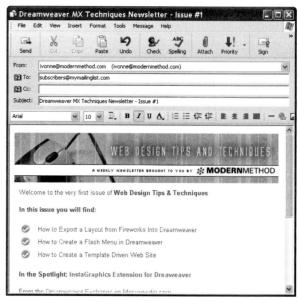

24.6

24.7

CREATING A FLOATING DHTML TOOLBAR

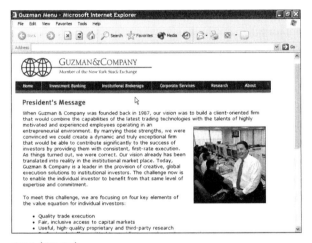

25.1 (CP 37)

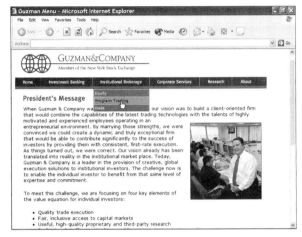

25.2 (CP 38)

If you're designing a site that requires various levels of menu navigation and don't want to clutter the body with second and third level toolbars, a great solution is to use a floating layer to build a menu that expands dynamically over the body of the page, as shown in **Figure 25.2 (CP 38)**. When the person's mouse moves away from the menu, the menu disappears automatically.

Many techniques exist to create a menu such as this one. I'll be the first to point out that this solution is not the most efficient when compared to those scripted from the ground up, or premade templates generated by software such as Fireworks. If you are comfortable editing JavaScript code, various hard-coded solutions are available all over the Web. A good place to start is the Macromedia Exchange site (`www.macromedia.com`), where various extensions produce crafty DHTML code for dynamic menus.

However, you will find that this technique is one of the easiest ways to build a custom DHTML menu with absolutely no code writing involved.

This technique is based on common table and layer commands, so it's also very easy to customize them to your liking.

STEP 1: INSERT YOUR MENU GRAPHICS

You can begin building your horizontal menu as you normally would. Many designers prefer to slice each button individually for rollover effects, which you can combine with the DHTML menu for added effect. This example uses a menu that already has rollover/rollout behaviors assigned.

- Create a new Web page with an image-based menu or use the Menu_Template.htm file provided on the CD-ROM. If you are new to creating image-based menus, please refer to Technique 12, "Building Rollovers in Fireworks and Exporting Them to Dreamweaver."
- Insert a value to both your left and top margin in the Page Properties dialog box by choosing **Modify ➢ Page Properties (Ctrl+J)**, even if the values are zero. Netscape and Internet Explorer have slightly different defaults for page margins, so this prevents your layers from appearing to be misaligned with your page.

TIP

If you want to import a single graphic for a menu, you can use an image map to create hot spots for both the links and the Layer behaviors outlined in the next section. See Technique 3 for more about image maps.

STEP 2: CREATE A SECOND LEVEL MENU TEMPLATE

- Choose **Insert ➢ Layer**. Resize the layer **100%** larger than your button. Center the layer to your button and position the top of the layer over your button.
- Click inside of the layer and then choose **Insert ➢ Table**.
- Create a three row, three column table. Merge the three cells on the first column into one large cell by using the **Merge Cells** button on the Property inspector. After the table is created, specify a width in pixels.
- Repeat the previous step on column three. The result is a table with five cells — two long ones on the sides and three in the center. Set the table border to **0** so that it is invisible beyond this point.
- Insert a one column, multiple row table in the center cell of the table. This nested table houses your menu links.
- Set a background color of your nested table or table rows/columns. This step is vital because your links can be difficult to read when overlapping the body content. You can also set the font color and size to improve their legibility.
- Insert some links into the rows of your nested tables. These links save you time when you copy and paste this template for your other menus.
- Position the layer to where the top of the first row of the nested table is flush with the button on your menu (see **Figure 25.3**). Dreamweaver may not show the same position as your Web browser — the best way to check if they are flush is to preview in your browser periodically as you design.

STEP 3: CREATE ALL MENU LAYERS

This step shows you how to create a foolproof parameter that hides your layer as soon as the mouse exits the submenu.

> **NOTE**
>
> This exercise assumes that your menu is left aligned and all of your layers have fixed left positioning. If your page is centered and you want to write your own code to support this, you will have to script the position of your layers dynamically with custom JavaScript. You can calculate this dynamic value of left by subtracting the browser resolution from the total width of your buttons area (usually the width of the table that houses them), and then adding the desired left position. You may also need to add page margins to your formula.

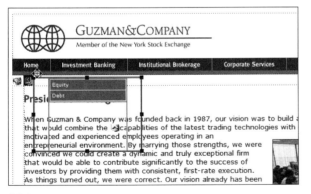

25.3

- Copy and paste the layer template you've created in the previous step until you have enough layers for all of the buttons for which you plan to show submenus.
- Position each layer accordingly so that the layer's location logically corresponds to the button. Please refer to **Figure 25.4** for an example.
- Give each layer a unique name. Your layer names should begin with a letter and contain no spaces. Unless you intend to show multiple layers at a time, the Z-index is not important. If you do, create your visibility hierarchy by setting higher numbers on the uppermost layers.
- Save and preview your work.

STEP 4: TURN LAYERS ON AND OFF

Now that all of your layers are in place, you must assign behaviors to your buttons to control their visibility. In addition, this step shows you how to use an invisible GIF to create a flexible parameter that hides your layer after the mouse moves away from the layer.

- Click one of your buttons. In this example, the button selected is "Investment Banking."

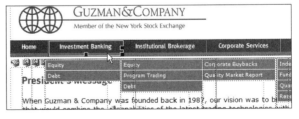

25.4

■ Click the **Plus Sign** (+) button in the Behaviors panel and choose **Show/Hide Layers**. The Show/Hide Layers dialog box appears.

■ Set the layer you want to show when this particular button is touched to **Show** (see **Figure 25.5**). Set every other layer to **Hide**. Repeat this step for all of the other buttons.

STEP 5: INSERT A SPACER GIF WITH BEHAVIORS

If you preview your work before this step, you should have layers that work like traffic lights — one turns on at a time but remains on until another one is called on. In other words, you need something to

hide the layers after they touch those empty cells you created in Step 2.

The invisible GIF, also known as a spacer GIF, is a one color graphic with the same color set to transparent so that it cannot be seen. The concept is to create an invisible border around each menu with these GIFs, assigning behaviors to them that hide the menus on mouse contact. This works because the mouse cannot move out of the menu area without going over one of these GIFs, triggering the Hide behavior.

■ Insert a spacer GIF into one of the blank cells.

■ Click the **Plus Sign** (+) button in the Behaviors panel and choose **Show/Hide Layers**. This time click and select all layers and hide every single one listed (see **Figure 25.6**). Click **OK** to close the dialog box.

■ Copy and paste this GIF into all empty cells you created. Size the GIF as needed.

■ Use the Vis menu in the Property inspector to set the visibility of all layers to hidden. Save and preview your work.

REMINDER

There is no limit to how many levels of menus you can create. Keep in mind your ideal page dimensions, because you don't want your menus going off the page on low-resolution displays. Please refer to the folder named Third_Level in the Technique 25 folder on the CD-ROM to view an example. I did this by inserting an arrow graphic as a button and followed the same steps listed previously. The only difference is that you have two layers set as Show for a third level button — the third level and the parent layer where the button resides.

TIP

Designating other common menu areas with hide-all functionality is also a good idea. For example, if the mouse touches the logo, you can hide all of the layers. This particular site has a logo graphic with a white background that spans the full length of the top menu, so moving anywhere beyond the top of the menu triggers the hide layers event. The spacer GIF is very versatile because you can size the hide-all perimeter to your needs. If you add more layers in the future, you can simply cut and paste it into those blank cells while retaining its hide-all properties. The only elements you have to tweak by hand are the buttons — hide the new layers you create accordingly.

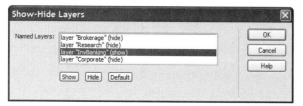

25.5

Your DHTML menu is complete as shown in **Figure 25.7**. You may need to fine-tune the size of your GIFs and your layer positions to get a pixel-perfect presentation.

NOTE

I encourage you to experiment with other solutions as soon as you grasp the theory behind this technique. For example, experiment with the OnBlur event instead of relying on the invisible GIF. Remember, you can also assign behaviors to blank cells — the invisible GIF is not a required component, but it does make the job easier.

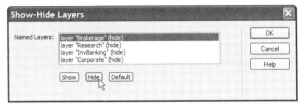

25.6

25.7

CHAPTER 6

DESIGNING FOR HIGH ACCESSIBILITY AND LOW BANDWIDTH

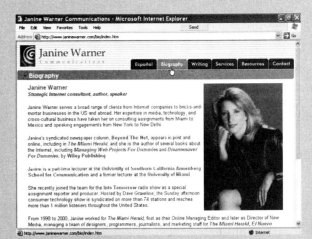

I f you want your Web site to reach the broadest possible audience, you can add features to enhance accessibility. Take into consideration visitors with disabilities who often use special browsers, as well as visitors with low bandwidth connections, especially important for sites that reach an international audience.

The techniques in this section aren't as flashy as some of the others, but they are easy to implement and may be the most valuable when it comes to ensuring that all of your visitors have a good experience on your Web site.

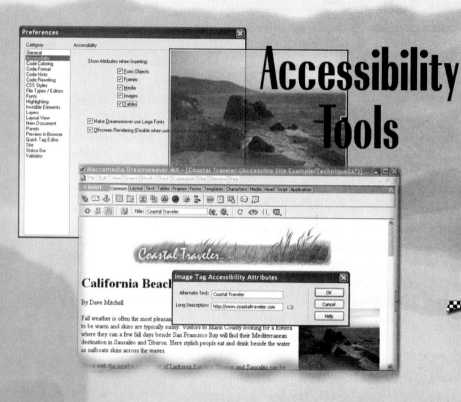

Accessibility Tools

ALT Tools

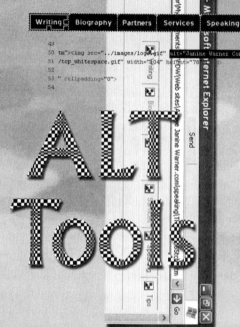

Preferences

Category
General
Accessibility
Code Coloring
Code Format
Code Hints
Code Rewriting
CSS Styles
File Types / Editors
Fonts
Highlighting
Invisible Elements
Layers
Layout View
New Document
Panels
Preview in Browser
Quick Tag Editor
Site
Status Bar
Validator

Accessibility

Show Attributes when Inserting:
- ☑ Form Objects
- ☑ Frames
- ☑ Media
- ☑ Images
- ☑ Tables

☑ Make Dreamweaver use Large Fonts
☑ Offscreen Rendering (Disable when us...)

Macromedia Dreamweaver MX - [Coastal Traveler (Accessible Site Example/Technique26")]
File Edit View Insert Modify Text Commands Site Window Help

Insert Common Layout Text Tables Frames Forms Templates Characters Media Head Script Application

Title: Coastal Traveler

Coastal Traveler

California Beach

By Dave Mitchell

Fall weather is often the most pleasant... to be warm and skies are typically sunny. Visitors to Marin County looking for a Riviera where they can a few fall days beside San Francisco Bay will find their Mediterranean destination in Sausalito and Tiburon. Here stylish people eat and drink beside the water as sailboats skim across the waves.

Along with the nearby... of Larkspur Landing, Tiburon and Sausalito can be

Image Tag Accessibility Attributes

Alternate Text: Coastal Traveler
Long Description: http://www.coastaltraveler.com

OK
Cancel
Help

```
49
50 tm"><img src="../images/logo.gif" alt="Janine Warner Communi
51 /top_whitespace.gif" width="104" height="78
52
53 " cellpadding="0">
54
```

Image
  Mode   ▶
  Adjust   ▶
  Duplicate...
  Apply Image...
  Calculations...
  Image Size...
  Canvas Size...
  Rotate Canvas ▶
  Crop
  Trim...
  Reveal All
  Histogram...
  Trap...
  Extract...   Alt+Ctrl+X
  Liquify...   Shft+Ctrl+X

  Bitmap
  Grayscale
  Duotone
  Indexed Color...
  ✔ RGB Color
  CMYK Color
  Lab Color
  Multichannel
  8 Bits/Channel
  16 Bits/Channel
  Color Table...
  Assign Profile...
  Convert to Profile...

...00% (RGB)

Low-Res

Navigation

Janine Warner Communications - Microsoft Internet Explorer
File Edit View Favorites Tools Help
Address http://www.janinewarner.com/bio/index.htm

Janine Warner
Communications

Espanol Biography Writing Ser... Resources Contact

Biography

Janine Warner
Strategic Internet consultant, author, speaker

Janine Warner serves a broad range of clients from Internet companies to bricks-and-mortar businesses in the US and abroad. Her expertise in media, technology, and cross-cultural business have taken her on consulting assignments from Miami to Mexico and speaking engagements from New York to New Delhi.

Janine... ...online, including... several books about the Internet, inc... *Dreamweaver For Dummies*, by Wiley Publishing

Janine is a part-time lecturer at the Unive... California Annenberg School for Communication and a former le... University of Miami.

She recently joined the team for the Into Tomo... show as a special assignment reporter and producer. Hosted by Dave Graveline, the Sunday afternoon consumer technology show is syndicated on more than 74 stations and reaches more than 1 million listeners throughout the United States.

From 1998 to 2000, Janine worked for *The Miami Herald*, first as their Online Managing Editor a... Director of New Media, managing a team of designers, programmers, journalists, and marketing staff for *The Miami Herald, El Nuevo*

http://www.janinewarner.com/bio/index.htm   Internet

Biography

USING DREAMWEAVER'S ACCESSIBILITY TOOLS

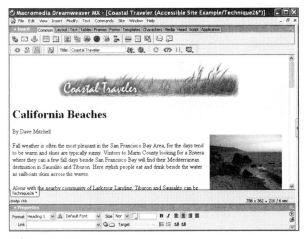

26.1 (CP 39)

26.2 (CP 40)

I f you're not sure about all of the elements you need to have on your Web pages to ensure they are accessible to visitors with disabilities, or you're just not sure you remembered to apply accessibility options to all of the elements on your pages, Dreamweaver's accessibility tools can help you double-check your work.

One of the key elements of accessible page design is that elements, such as multimedia files, as associated with labels and descriptions can be "read" by special browsers. When you activate Dreamweaver's accessibility features in preferences, special dialog boxes appear to remind you to add accessibility elements, such as the one shown in **Figure 26.2 (CP 40)**.

STEP 1: ACTIVATE DREAMWEAVER'S ACCESSIBILITY TOOLS

Before you can use Dreamweaver's accessibility tools, you need to activate them in Preferences.

■ Choose **Edit ➢ Preferences** and select **Accessibility** to reveal these options, as shown in **Figure 26.3**.

■ Place a checkmark in each box to activate the feature. You can choose to activate any or all of the

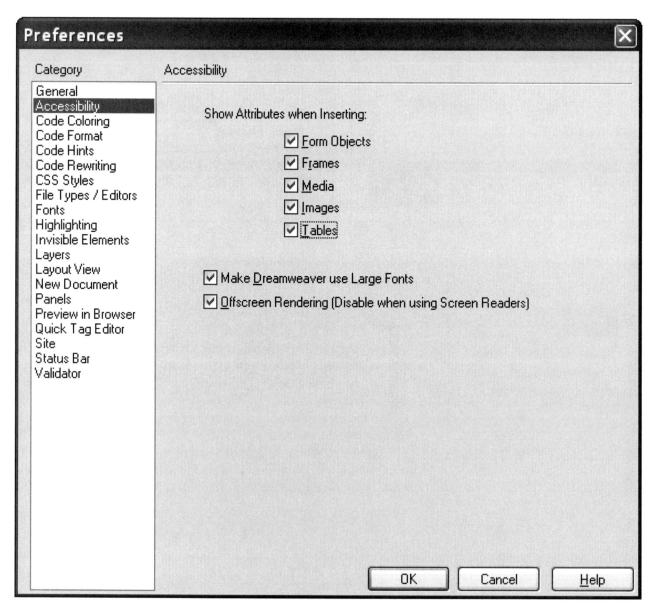

26.3

accessibility tools. You must restart Dreamweaver for this change to take effect.

STEP 2: USING ACCESSIBILITY TOOLS

■ After you activate these options, you are prompted to add the necessary elements, such as the Alternate Text and Long Description shown in **Figure 26.4**.

■ If you create a page that uses Frames, you'll be prompted to name each frame to make it accessible.

■ Multimedia objects, such as video clips and Flash files, also have accessibility attributes.

> **TIP**
>
> Dreamweaver has a number of features built-in that make it more accessible to use by anyone with disabilities. For example, you can set up key commands to use the keyboard to navigate Dreamweaver's floating panels, Property inspector, dialog boxes, and more.

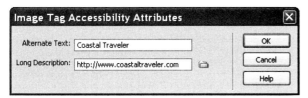

26.4

> **TIP**
>
> In addition to editing alternative attributes in the Tag Code Editor, you can edit the text directly in Code View (but only if you really know what you're doing).

When you insert these elements on your pages, Dreamweaver prompts you for the appropriate alternative information. To edit accessibility values for media objects, right-click (Windows) or ⌘-click (Mac) and choose **Edit Tag Code**.

■ Form elements, such as radio buttons and text fields, also have accessibility attributes. When you insert form elements on your pages, Dreamweaver prompts you for the appropriate alternative information. To edit accessibility values for form elements, right-click (Windows) or ⌘-click (Mac) and choose **Edit Tag Code**.

> **REMINDER**
>
> Many government organizations and non-profits require that Web sites be accessible to all potential users. As part of the Americans with Disabilities Act, if your group or agency receives government funds, you could be required to comply with accessible Web design techniques.

PROVIDING MULTIPLE NAVIGATION OPTIONS

27.1 (CP 41)

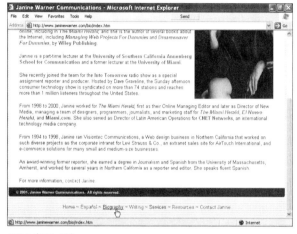

27.2 (CP 42)

Providing text navigation elements, such as the one shown in **Figure 27.2 (CP 42)**, is one of the simplest ways to make your Web pages more accessible to those with disabilities, as well as those limited by slow connections. The images with the rollover effect shown in **Figure 27.1 (CP 41)** provide an excellent design option and intuitive user interface, but those images take longer to load than text and won't be visible to everyone. Even if you provide alternative text behind your images, as described in Technique 26, providing a list of text links at the bottom of your pages is a commonly recognized alternative to graphic options and saves viewers time and effort.

STEP 1: CREATE A TEXT NAVIGATION ROW

- Type to enter a text description for each of the pages you link to in your navigation row.
- Separating each word or phrase with a non-text element, such as the vertical bar (|) or the tilde (~) is good.

- Create links for each of the words or phrases as you would for images in a navigation bar. If you use one big image and want to create an image map, Technique 3 in Chapter 1 shows you how.
- Save the text navigation row as a part of a template or as a library element to make it easy to place on multiple pages. (See Technique 38 in Chapter 8 to find out how to use templates for this purpose.)

STEP 2: MAKE A TEXT NAVIGATION ROW A LIBRARY ITEM

- After you type in the navigation row and set all of the links, click the **Assets** tab in the Files panel

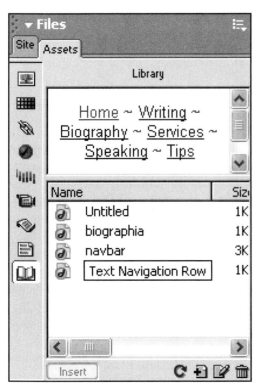

27.3

and select the **Library** icon from the bottom left, as shown in **Figure 27.3**.

- Click to highlight the entire navigation row, as shown in **Figure 27.4**, and drag it onto the Library Assets panel. It automatically is added as a library item.
- Name the library item something you'll remember when you need it next. I've named mine Text Navigation Row, as shown in Figure 27.3. You can click and drag it from the library onto any other page to add the navigation row.

See **Figure 27.5** for the navigation row on a Web site.

> **REMINDER**
>
> Dreamweaver's template and library items features offer the added benefit that if you ever edit them, the change is automatically applied to every page where that library item is used or the template is applied. This is especially useful for elements, such as navigation bars, which appear on every page on a Web site and often need to be changed when you add, remove, or alter new sections of a site.

Home ~ Writing ~ Biography ~ Services ~ Speaking ~ Tips

27.4

Home ~ Español ~ Biography ~ Writing ~ Services ~ Resources ~ Contact Janine

27.5

USING ALT TAGS TO DESCRIBE IMAGES

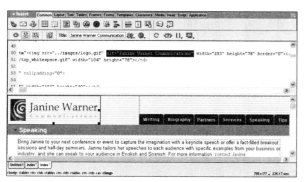

28.1

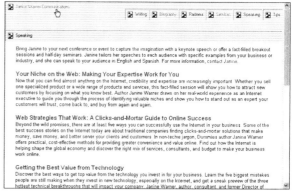

28.2

Alt text is one of the simplest and most important HTML attributes, but it's also one of the easiest to forget to include because it is included "behind" an image, where it is not visible to most viewers. If you use the Internet Explorer browser, the Alt text appears when you move your cursor over an image, as shown in **Figure 28.2,** but it is otherwise invisible when images are displayed.

Alt text is important when someone views your pages with the images turned off or uses a browser that does not display images. (Yes, there really are browsers that don't display images.) And Alt text is crucial for visitors who are blind or visually impaired and use text browsers or readers because Alt tags provide alternative text that can be "read" by special browsers for the visually impaired. If you use images for buttons or other text information, Alt text is especially important because without the alternative text description, the meaning of buttons is lost to these users.

As Web pages are viewed on more and more devices, such as handheld computers and even cell phones with very small screens, Alt text becomes important for new reasons because many of these small devices use text-only browsers that only pick up the text on a page.

STEP 1: INSERT ALT TEXT

Alt text is simply a word or short description that is included in the code that inserts an image on a page. If an image is not visible in a browser, the Alt text displays in its place. If a visitor uses a special browser to "read" the page out loud, Alt text is read in place of the image.

Dreamweaver makes it easy to include Alt text: Simply type in the text you want as an alternative in the Property inspector.

To add Alt text to an image, follow these steps:

- Insert an image or select an image that has already been inserted on a page (see **Figure 28.3**). Notice that after you select an image, the Property inspector displays the image properties.
- In the top right of the Property inspector, enter the text you want to provide as an alternative behind your image in the Alt text box (see **Figure 28.4**).
- The alternative text is automatically inserted in the Image tag in the source code.

| Writing | Biography | Partners | Services | Speaking |

28.3

STEP 2: LOOK FOR MISSING ALT TAGS

It's easy to forget to include Alt tags when you're developing a Web page. You don't see them, and the page works perfectly in most browsers without them. Here are three ways to look for missing Alt text.

- You can select any image and view the Alt text area of the Property inspector to see if the alternative text has already been included. If not, simply type it into the text field in the Property inspector.
- If you use the Internet Explorer browser, you can turn off images so that they don't display. The Alt text is then visible in the browser window, or not visible if no Alt text is included. This method makes it easy to see all the missing Alt text on a page with one glance. To turn off images in Internet Explorer, choose **Tools ➢ Internet**

REMINDER

You can enter any text you want as alternative text behind an image, but, in general, it's best to keep it brief and focus on a description that would be useful to someone who can't see the image. For example, if the image is a Contact Us button, you can simply include Contact Us as the alternative text. If the image is a photo or complex design with no words, consider including a brief description.

Options and then click the **Advanced** tab. Under Accessibility, place a check next to **Always expand ALT text for images**. Under Multimedia, remove the checkmark next to **Show pictures**.

■ Use Dreamweaver's Accessibility Validation tools, described in more detail in Technique 26

earlier in this chapter, to automatically check for missing Alt text. To generate a report that includes a list of all images without Alt Tags, choose **File ➢ Check Page ➢ Check Accessibility**.

See **Figure 28.5** for a Web page with Alt text.

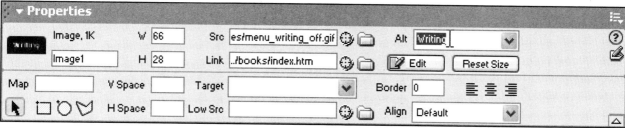

28.4

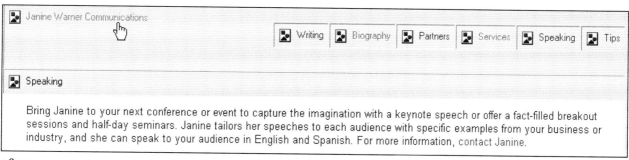

28.5

INSERTING A QUICK-LOADING LOW-RES IMAGE

29.1

I f you want to offer big, beautiful images on your Web pages but don't want to lose visitors who get impatient waiting for them to download over a slow connection, consider using a *low-res* image. Here's how it works: You insert a low-resolution image, which is smaller in file size, at the same time that you insert the high-resolution version — in the next section, you see how easy this is to do when you use Dreamweaver. When your page loads, the low-res image loads first, and if you make it a small file size, it pops right into place. Then, the high-res image slowly appears over the low-res image, depending on how long it takes for the high-res version to download.

Not only is this a great trick for low bandwidth users, but it can also create a cool effect as the high-resolution image replaces the low-resolution version. One of my favorite uses of this trick is to take a color photograph, such as the one shown in **Figure 29.1** and create a black-and-white version to serve as the low-res version. Black-and-white works well for low-res because when you strip out the color, you end up with a much smaller file size, even though it's exactly the same physical dimension. Not only does this create the illusion that the page loads more quickly, it creates a cool effect when the black-and-white image slowly transforms into a color one. To give you an idea about how much smaller the file size can be when you strip out the color, the low-resolution, black-and-white version is only 4.5K, while the high-resolution, color version is four times the size at 20K.

STEP 1: CREATE A LOW-RES IMAGE

The simplest way I've found to create a low-res version of a color photograph, such as the one used in this example, is to open the color image in a program such as Adobe Photoshop and change the image from color to grayscale. To do this, choose **Image ➢ Mode ➢ Grayscale**, as shown in **Figure 29.2**. As soon as you have two versions of the image, use the following steps to insert the high-res and low-res versions in Dreamweaver.

> **NOTE**
>
> Not all browsers support this feature, but if the browser used to view your page does not support low-res images, it displays the high-res version only.

You insert a low-resolution image in Dreamweaver just as you insert a high-resolution version. I recommend that you insert the high-resolution version first and then add the low-resolution version. Follow these steps to do so.

- Choose **Insert ➢ Image** and browse to find the image. As soon as the image loads on the page, click to select the image so that the image properties are visible in the Property inspector.

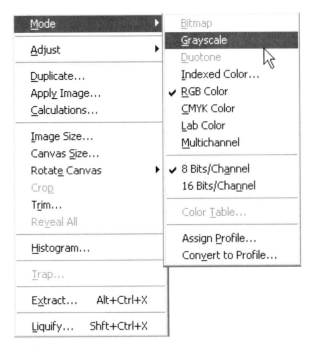

29.2

- If you want to add a low-res version to an existing image, simply click to select an image that has already been inserted on a page. Notice that when an image is selected, the Property inspector displays the image properties.

- In the bottom of the Property inspector, just under Target, you find a text box labeled Low. Use the **Browse** button to the right of the Low text box, shown in **Figure 29.3**, to find the image you want to use as the low-res version. (The Browse buttons in Dreamweaver all look like small file folders.)

- After you select the low-res version, you should see the high-resolution version in the Src area of the Property inspector and the low-res version in the Low area of the Property inspector.

- Save your work and preview it in a browser to see the effect.

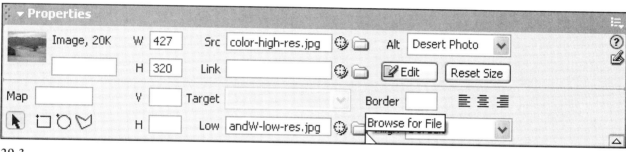

29.3

CHAPTER 7

IMAGE TRICKS THAT MAKE YOU LOOK GOOD

P erforming the simple techniques that follow can quickly add style and life to your Web pages. You should be familiar with rollovers and layers to work through the techniques in this chapter.

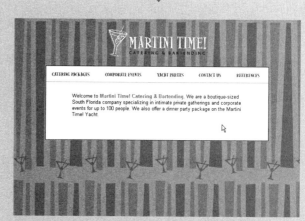

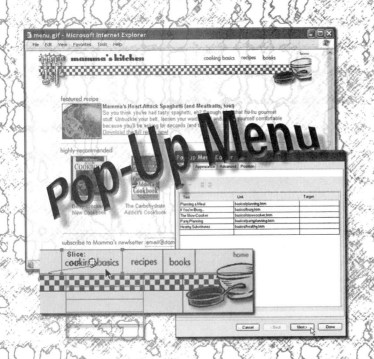

Pop-Up Menu

AUTOSTRETCH

CITY SUMMER CAMP

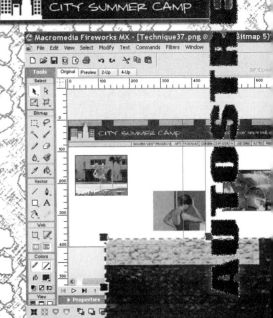

Slideshow

Zooming In

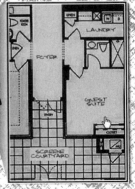

"ZOOMING IN" WITH ROLLOVERS

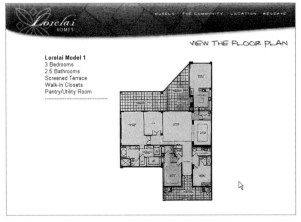

30.1 (CP 43)

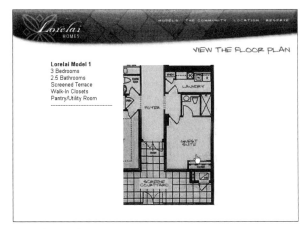

30.2 (CP 44)

For this technique, use the files in the Technique 30 folder on the CD-ROM. For an example of this technique, open the file called zoom_finished.htm in the Technique 30 folder.

This technique combines rollovers (see Technique 2) and image maps (see Technique 3). When you mouse over a certain part of the image map shown in **Figure 30.1 (CP 43)**, it appears to be zooming in to that area of the image, as shown in **Figure 30.2 (CP 44)**.

STEP 1: PREPARE THE MAIN IMAGE AND THE ROLLOVER ZOOM-IN IMAGES IN A GRAPHICS EDITING PROGRAM

When creating a "zoom-in" rollover, your original image and all zoomed-in images should be the same width and height as the original image so that it covers the same space. In this technique, I use Adobe Photoshop to prepare the images, but the steps are similar in other graphics editing programs, such as Macromedia Fireworks or Corel Photo-Paint. If you are using the files from the CD-ROM and prefer to skip this step, a set of zoomed-in images are also available on the CD-ROM in the "images" subfolder of Technique 30.

- Choose **File ➢ Open** and browse to find original.gif.
- Reduce the image to 25% of its original size and save it as zoom.gif. This is the starting image on your page. Leave this file open in your graphics program.

- Copy sections of the original.gif file and paste them into the zoom.gif file, saving each new section as a separate file with a descriptive name, such as "master_suite.gif" and "livingroom.gif." See **Figure 30.3**. This method of copying and pasting ensures that all your rollover image files are the same width and height as zoom.gif.

STEP 2: INSERT STARTING IMAGE INTO WEB PAGE

In Dreamweaver, you now insert the starting image into its position on your Web page.

- Open the page you want to use. If using the files from the CD-ROM, this page is called Technique30.htm.
- Insert the starting image.

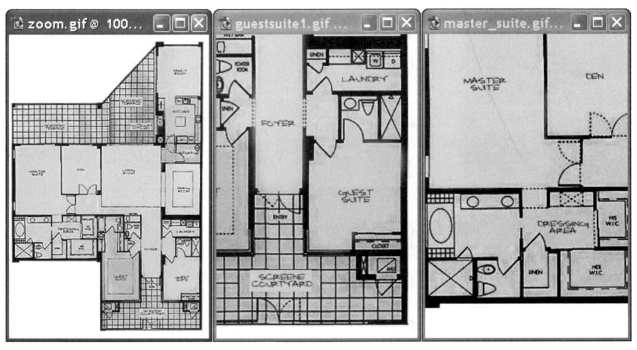

30.3

STEP 3: CREATE THE IMAGE MAP

- Using the **Image Map Shape** tools, mark off each area of the image that you "zoom" into, making sure not to overlap any of the areas. You should know beforehand what areas you want for zooming in, because you created all the zoomed-in images prior to starting any work in Dreamweaver. See **Figure 30.4**.

STEP 4: ADD ROLLOVER ACTION

- Click the **Image Map Selection** arrow and click one of the highlighted areas of the image map.
- In the Behaviors panel, click the **Plus Sign** (+) button and choose **Swap Image** from the menu.
- Click the **Browse** button to find the zoomed in image that corresponds with the selected area. Choose it and click **OK**. Then, click **OK** to close the Swap Image dialog box. Follow this step for every selected area on the image map.

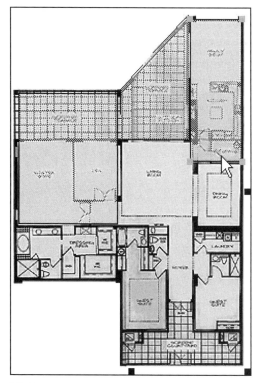

30.4

STEP 5: TEST THE ZOOM-IN ACTION

■ Preview the page in your browser and mouse over the image. Different areas of the image should zoom in depending on where you place your mouse. See **Figure 30.5**.

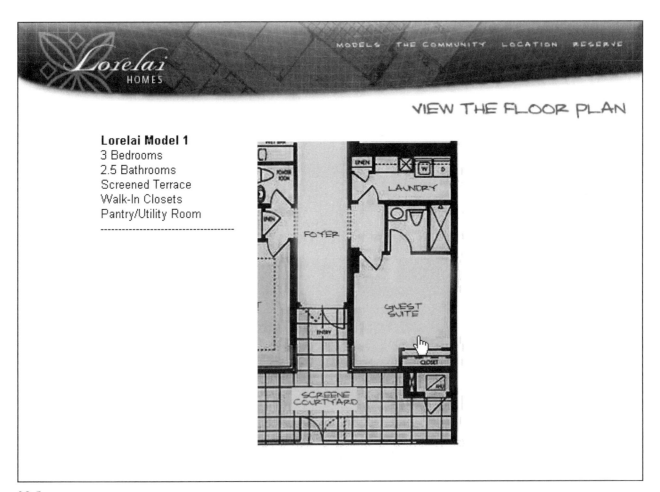

30.5

EDITING IMAGES FROM WITHIN DREAMWEAVER

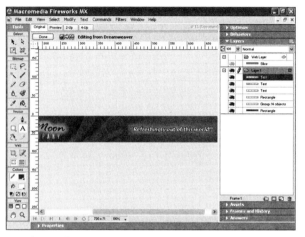

31.1 (CP 45)

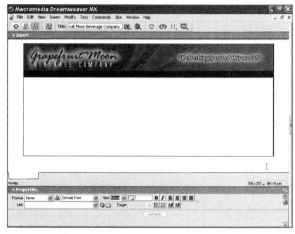

31.2 (CP 46)

NOTE

For this technique, use the files in the Technique 31 folder on the CD-ROM. You find a page called Technique31.htm and a Fireworks file called Technique31.png.

I f you created your graphics in Fireworks — and even if you haven't! — you can edit your graphics later from within Dreamweaver. As soon as you slice up your layout and begin working in Dreamweaver, if you change your mind about a graphic, it's as simple as clicking the Edit button. See **Figure 31.1 (CP 45)** for the graphic in Fireworks and **Figure 31.2 (CP 46)** for the graphic in Dreamweaver.

STEP 1: SELECT THE IMAGE YOU WANT TO EDIT

The file you are going to edit in this technique was created in Fireworks; therefore, the JPEG in the Dreamweaver document has a corresponding .png file.

- In Dreamweaver, choose **File ➤ Open** and browse to find Technique31.htm.
- Select the title image, header.jpg (see **Figure 31.3**).
- In the Property inspector, click **Edit**. This launches the Fireworks application.
- The first time you edit a file directly from the Dreamweaver document, Fireworks displays a dialog box asking if you want to use an existing Fireworks file as the source for this image. In this case, there is a Fireworks file available: technique31.png. Click **Yes** and browse for this .png file to open it in Fireworks.

STEP 2: EDIT THE IMAGE IN FIREWORKS

- With the source file open in Fireworks, make a change on the graphic. In this example, I am going to add a tagline next to the logo.
- When you are satisfied with your changes, click **Done** at the top of the Fireworks screen. See **Figure 31.4**. The updated image appears automatically in Dreamweaver as shown in **Figure 31.5**.

> **NOTE**
>
> If you don't have a source file or you do have one but prefer to edit the actual image instead of the source file, click **No**, keeping in mind that any changes you make to this image are permanent.

> **NOTE**
>
> If you are editing a Fireworks file that was created on another computer, you might not have the fonts used in that file. In such a case, Fireworks asks you if you want to Maintain Appearance or Change Fonts. If you select Maintain Appearance, the layout continues to show the text in the missing font. If you choose to edit the type, however, you will lose the original appearance and will be asked to select another font. If you choose Change Fonts, Fireworks asks you to select another font from your system to use in place of the missing font.

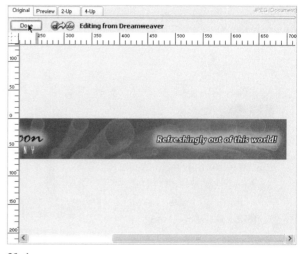

31.4

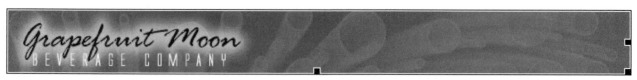

31.3

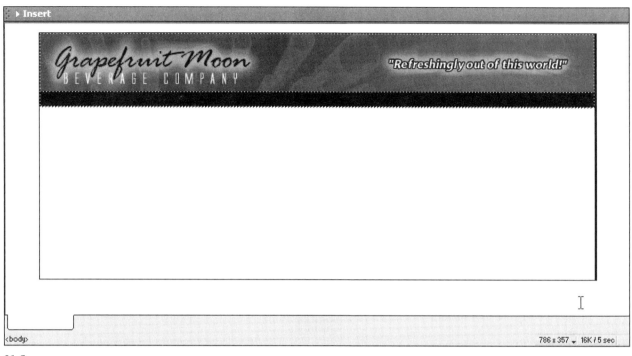

31.5

BUILDING A POP-UP MENU
USING FIREWORKS

32.1

32.2

NOTE

For this technique, use the files in the Technique 32 folder on the CD-ROM. You find a Fireworks file called Technique32_start.png and a finished example of the technique called Technique32_finished.htm.

This technique achieves a similar result to that achieved in Technique 25, "Create a Floating DHTML Toolbar," but it is done using Macromedia Fireworks. After you create your layout in Fireworks, adding a pop-up menu is a piece of cake. The result is a very accessible Web site with a highly professional appearance. See **Figure 32.2**.

You can save a lot of time if you take a moment to plan your Web site navigation before starting this technique with your own project. In this example, you work with a recipe Web site called Mamma's Kitchen. The navigation consists of three major sections: Cooking Basics, Recipes, and Books. You use Fireworks to create the navigation for the site. Under Cooking Basics will be various links to information on meal planning, healthy cooking alternatives, and tips for busy people. The Recipes menu links to such categories as Appetizers, Soups 'n' Salads, Main Course, Side Dishes, and such. The Books button won't have a pop-up menu.

STEP 1: OPEN YOUR SOURCE FILE

■ In Fireworks, choose **File ➤ Open** and browse to find Technique32_start.png. In this example, the graphics and slices are already done for you.

STEP 2: ADD THE POP-UP MENU

■ Click the slice over Cooking Basics.
■ Choose **Modify ➤ Pop-Up Menu ➤ Add Pop-Up Menu**. The Pop-Up Menu Editor appears (see **Figure 32.3**).

> **NOTE**
>
> Fireworks also opens layout files created with Photoshop, which you can then save as .png files.

■ Under the Content tab, click the **Plus Sign** (+) button to add a menu item, and then enter the name of the first link you want to have appear on the pop-up menu. Tab once to move the cursor to the next text box over. In this text box, enter the URL for this menu item. If you want the linked URL to open up in a new browser window, tab over once more and choose **_blank** from the list.
■ Click **Next** to move to the next tab.
■ Under the Appearance tab, you can determine what you want your menu to look like. You have options for creating the menu in HTML or as images, and vertical or horizontal. In this step you can determine the typeface and size and the background and text color of the on and off states. Refer to **Figure 32.4** to see what I did.
■ Click **Next** to move to the next tab.

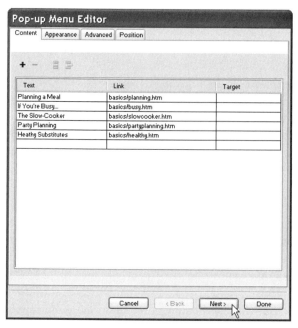

32.3

32.4

32.5

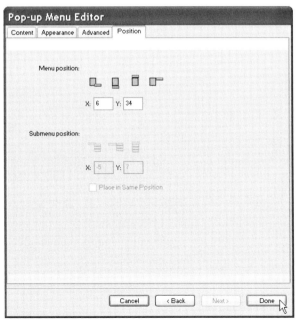

32.6

- Under the Advanced tab — which sounds scarier than it really is — you can define the amount of cell spacing in each menu item, the color of the border, and whether or not you want a border to show. See **Figure 32.5**.
- Click **Next** to move to the next tab.
- Under the Position tab, you can determine how you align the menu in relation to the slice. See **Figure 32.6**. In this example, I aligned it to the bottom of the slice and then played with the exact X- and Y-positioning so that the menu appears to be left-aligned with the text in each slice.
- Click **Done**. If you click one of the slices now, you see an outline of the pop-up menu (see **Figure 32.7**). Notice the behaviors listed in the Behaviors panel: onMouseOver and Show Popup Menu (see **Figure 32.8**).

32.7

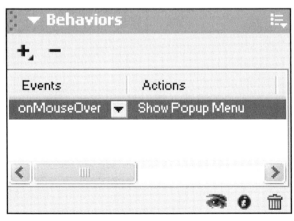

32.8

STEP 3: EXPORT YOUR LAYOUT

■ After determining the properties for each slice, choose **File** ➤ **Export**. Save your HTML file as menu.htm. See Technique 4 in Chapter 1 for more on exporting a layout from Fireworks. You can also use the file called menu.htm, available on the CD-ROM.

STEP 4: COMPLETE YOUR LAYOUT IN DREAMWEAVER

■ In Dreamweaver, open the new HTML file you created in Fireworks (or menu.htm from the CD-ROM) and the file called Technique32_

start.htm. To complete your layout, you insert the newly created navigation from menu.htm into Technique32_start.htm.
■ In Design View, select all the contents from menu.htm and copy it.
■ Switch to Technique32_start.htm and position the cursor on the empty cell at the top of that table. Paste into that cell. The contents of menu.htm appear on this page. See **Figure 32.9**.
■ Preview this page in your browser. To see an example of the finished page, open the CD-ROM file called Technique32_finished.htm in your browser. See **Figure 32.10**.

32.9

mamma's kitchen

cooking basics   recipes   books

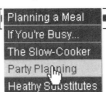

Planning a Meal
If You're Busy...
The Slow-Cooker
Party Planning
Heathy Substitutes

featured recipe

Mamma's Heart-Attack Spaghetti (and Meatballs, too!)
So you think you've had tasty spaghetti, eh? Enough of all that fru-fru gourmet stuff. Unbuckle your belt, loosen your waist band and make yourself comfortable because you'll be asking for seconds (and thirds!).
Download the full recipe now!

highly-recommended

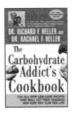

Betty Crocker's
New Cookbook

The Carbohydrate
Addict's Cookbook

How to Cook
Everything

Betty Crocker's
Ultimate Cake Mix
Cookbook

subscribe to Mamma's newlsetter email@domain.com Submit

32.10

CREATING A SLIDESHOW USING THE TIMELINE AND BEHAVIORS

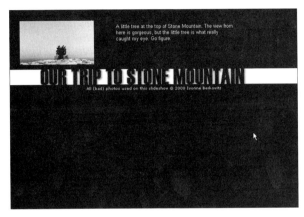

33.1

I f Flash isn't available to you, alternatively you can create a DHTML slideshow by using the timeline and behaviors in Dreamweaver. In this technique, you create a three-photo slideshow by using photos from my trip to Stone Mountain in Georgia. See **Figure 33.1**. The first image slides in and a caption appears to the right. After five seconds, that image slides out to the left as the second image slides in and *its* caption appears. After another five seconds, the second image slides out to the left and the third and final image slides in with its accompanying text. Finally, a black layer slides in from the top saying, "The End."

STEP 1: INSERT LAYERS FOR FIRST PHOTO AND CAPTION

- Open a new page in Dreamweaver.
- Choose **Insert ➢ Layers** to insert a new layer into your document. Name this layer Photo1. Inside the layer, insert the image called

photo1.jpg (choose **Insert ➤ Image**). Make this layer 200 pixels wide by 115 pixels high. You can select the layer and enter these values in the Property inspector.

■ Choose **Insert ➤ Layers** to insert another layer. Name this layer Photo1Text. This layer holds the caption for Photo 1. You can type some amusing descriptive text about Photo1 here. Make this layer 331 pixels wide by 115 pixels high. This layer should also be hidden. To hide this layer, choose **Hidden** from the Vis menu in the Property inspector. The Top position for both layers should be 29 pixels. Enter this value for each layer in the Property inspector next to "T."

STEP 2: ADD LAYER MOTION USING THE TIMELINE

■ Choose **Window ➤ Others ➤ Timelines Panel** to view the Timelines panel.

■ Click **View ➤ Visual Aids ➤ Invisible Elements** to make sure you can see the yellow marker for the Photo1 layer. Then, right-click Frame 1 of Row 1 on the timeline. From the menu that appears, choose **Add Object**. This places a beginning and ending keyframe on the timeline.

NOTE

When working with layers, you can make them any size you want in Dreamweaver. The sizes I specify for the layers created in this technique are just a personal preference to accommodate the size of the images with which I'm working.

■ Drag the ending keyframe to Frame 15. Your active frames should start on Frame 1 and end on Frame 15 now.

■ Select the Photo1 layer again and then click Frame 1. Use your arrow key to nudge the frame to the left until it is not visible; alternatively, type –203 as the L value in the Property inspector. Click the playhead above Frame 1 and drag to move it across the timeline to Frame 15. The Photo1 layer now moves smoothly onto the page from the left.

■ Release the playhead and move your mouse cursor over to Frame 90. Because the frames animate at a rate of 15 frames per second, this causes the Photo1 layer to remain in that position for five seconds. Click Frame 90 and then reselect the layer by clicking the yellow marker. Right-click Frame 90 and again select **Add Object**.

■ Drag the ending keyframe to Frame 105. Your second set of active frames start on Frame 90 and end on Frame 105 now. You are going to create an exit animation for the Photo1 layer.

■ Select the Photo1 layer again and then click Frame 105. Use your arrow key to nudge the frame to the left until it is not visible; alternatively, type –203 again as the L value in the Property inspector. Click the playhead above Frame 90 and drag

---

NOTE

The markers aren't always in the expected order on your document. You can click a layer's yellow marker and then use the Property inspector to verify that you have chosen the correct layer.

to move it across the timeline to Frame 105. The Photo1 layer now moves smoothly to the left and *out* of the page.

STEP 3: ADD BEHAVIORS TO SHOW AND HIDE TEXT LAYERS

■ Select the Photo1 layer on your document and click Frame 15 on the row labeled B above all the other rows. See **Figure 33.2**. In the Behaviors tab, click the **Plus Sign** (+) button and choose **Show/Hide Layers** from the menu. In the Show-Hide Layers dialog box (see **Figure 33.3**), select **Photo1Text** and click **Show**. Click **OK**.

> ### NOTE
>
> Repeat Steps 1–3 to add the other two photos and "The End" slide to the slideshow. See the finished file on the CD-ROM, Technique33_ finished.htm, as a guide.

■ On the timeline, move your mouse cursor over and click Frame 105 and also the row labeled B. In the Behaviors panel, click the **Plus Sign** (+) button and select **Show/Hide Layers** from the menu. In the Show-Hide Layers dialog box, select **Photo1Text** and click **Hide**. Click **OK**.

STEP 4: PREVIEW IN YOUR BROWSER

■ Make sure that the Autoplay check box is checked, and press **F12** to preview your slideshow in your default browser. The animation should move along as described in the beginning of this technique.

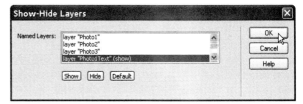

33.3

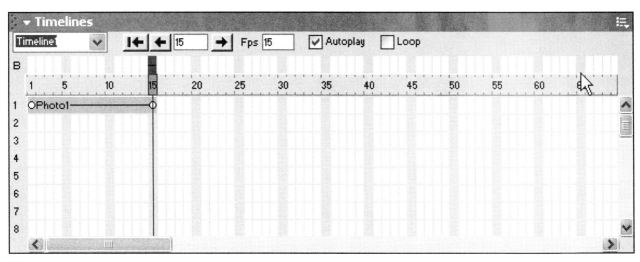

33.2

ADDING STYLE TO YOUR PAGE WITH A FIXED TILING BACKGROUND

34.1 (CP 47)

34.2 (CP 48)

NOTE

For this technique, use the files in the Technique 34 folder on the CD-ROM.

A good Web designer knows that sometimes a solid color background just doesn't cut it — see **Figure 34.1 (CP 47)**. For those times, a seamless, tiling background does the trick, adding an element of style and personality to an otherwise bland Web page, as shown in **Figure 34.2 (CP 48)**.

STEP 1: CREATE THE ELEMENTS FOR THE TILING BACKGROUND IN FIREWORKS

■ In Fireworks, choose **File ➢ New** to create a new document at 300 by 800 pixels. Alternately, you can browse the CD-ROM to find the file called Technique34.png, which is already done for you.

■ Use any combination of drawing tools to draw various shapes until you are satisfied with the design or pattern. Keep in mind that the final size of the tiling background image used as an example will be 190 pixels wide by 420 pixels high, though you can make your tiling backgrounds any size.

■ Choose **Modify ➤ Symbol ➤ Convert to Symbol**. In the Symbol Properties dialog box, select **Graphic** and click **OK**.

STEP 2: CREATE THE TILING BACKGROUND

■ Position your symbol at X=**0** and Y=**0** using the Property inspector.

■ Select your symbol and choose **Edit ➤ Clone** to make a new layer with a copy of the symbol. Select this clone and type X=**190** and Y=**0**.

■ Click the symbol at the 0,0 position to select it. Holding the **Shift** key, click the clone next to it. With both items selected, choose **Edit ➤ Clone** to create a copy of each one.

■ Make sure these two new copies are selected and move them down to a Y-position of **420** by using the Property inspector.

■ Use the **Crop** tool to crop this image down to 190 x 420 pixels (see **Figure 34.3**). You can tweak the width and height of the crop marquee by typing in exact pixel measurements in the Property inspector (see **Figure 34.4**).

■ When you are satisfied with your tiling background, you can export the image by choosing **File ➤ Export**.

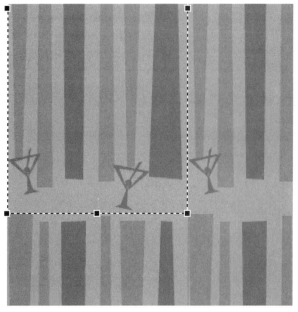

34.3

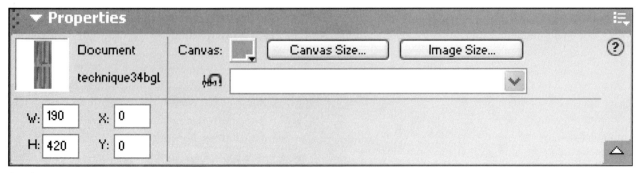

34.4

STEP 3: ADD TILING BACKGROUND TO YOUR WEB PAGE IN DREAMWEAVER

■ Start Dreamweaver and open the file to which you will add the tiling background. You can use the file called Technique34_nobackground.htm on the CD-ROM.

■ Choose **Modify ➢ Page Properties**. In the Page Properties dialog box, browse for the image you just exported from Fireworks. On the CD-ROM, this file is called tilingbg_short.gif. Select your file and click **OK**. Your background now tiles across the Web page. See **Figure 34.5**.

34.5

TILE STYLE

I f you prefer to have an area of solid color toward the bottom of the tile, instead of having the pattern repeat immediately, you can do this in one of two ways. With the newer browsers, you can create a style for the body that specifies no vertical tiling. For older browsers, you can make the tile longer, for example, 800 pixels high. And only clone and nudge to the right, omitting the last part of Step 2. See the following figure and Technique34Alternative.htm on the CD-ROM for an example.

PREVENTING BACKGROUNDS FROM TILING AND SCROLLING

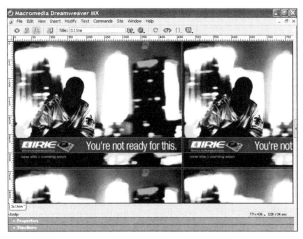

35.1 (CP 49)

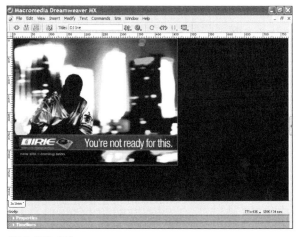

35.2 (CP 50)

One of the many uncertainties of Web design is that you never really know in what screen resolution a person will view your sites. When it comes to inserting full-bleed graphical backgrounds, many designers make a big picture that tiles off the screen. This technique has one major drawback—it can create a large file that will take too long to load. You also are limited to how much content you can put on a given page, because too much causes the background to scroll again. The best is to explicitly define background properties with CSS, or Cascading Style Sheets, so that there is no guessing involved.

If you set the background property of the page by using Dreamweaver's standard method, the background tiles by default, as shown in **Figure 35.1 (CP 49)**. This behavior is predicted in HTML. However, you can use an alternative method by using Style Sheets, which not only prevent the background from tiling, but also from scrolling off-screen, as shown in **Figure 35.2 (CP 50)**.

STEP 1: CREATE A STYLE SHEET

■ Create a new Web page. Because you'll be inserting an image, be sure to save your page before proceeding.

■ Choose **Text ➤ CSS Styles ➤ New CSS Style** to open the New CSS Style dialog box.

■ Select the **Redefine HTML** radio button. The form field at the top of the dialog box changes to a pull-down menu. Click to select the <body> tag. If this background is going to be shared throughout the site, select (**New Style Sheet File**) or an existing style sheet located in your site under the Define menu. Otherwise, select **This Document Only**.

TIP

If you want your background to stay on-screen while the page scrolls, choose **Fixed** from the Attachment menu. If your page has only a little bit of content but you want to see what a fixed property background does, simply press the Enter key several times to create a longer page. This choice keeps the background locked in its place on the browser even while the page is being scrolled.

NOTE

Some older Web browsers do not support CSS, such as Internet Explorer 3.

STEP 2: DEFINE YOUR BACKGROUND

■ The CSS Style definition for body dialog box appears (see **Figure 35.3**). By default, Type is selected. Click **Background** to change the dialog box options.

■ Click the **Browse** button to choose a Background Image. Select your file and click **OK**. Choose **no-repeat** from the Repeat menu.

■ Click **OK** to close the CSS Style definition dialog box. Click **Done** to close the Edit Style Sheet dialog box.

Your background now appears without tiling, as shown in **Figure 35.4**. Save and test in your Web browser.

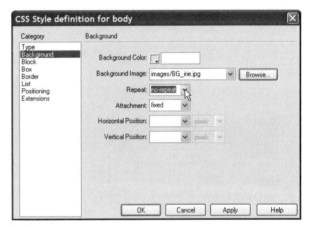

35.3

35.4

CREATING TILING GRAPHICS FOR USE IN AUTOSTRETCH LAYOUTS

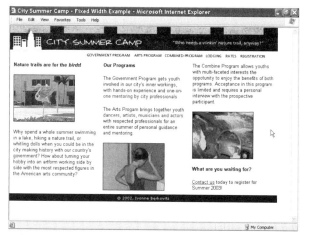

36.1

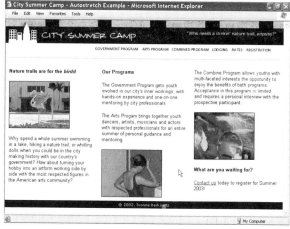

36.2

Often, the best way to display the most information possible on any user's Web browser is to create an autostretch layout. This means the layout stretches to the width of the browser window. This is also a quick and easy way to make a Web page more visually appealing if there is too much empty space — not that too much empty space is *always* a bad thing, from a design perspective! See **Figures 36.1** and **36.2**.

STEP 1: PREPARE AND SLICE YOUR LAYOUT IN A GRAPHICS PROGRAM

I provide both a Fireworks .png file and a Photoshop .psd file for your convenience. Notice the background of the header/title area is a repeating pattern of a yellow dashed line on a road.

■ Slice your layout for exporting to HTML. In this example, I use Fireworks to export to HTML. See **Figure 36.3** for an example of a properly sliced layout. You can also use Adobe ImageReady to perform this step, or you can do it manually. The HTML file called Technique36.htm shows the layout exported from Fireworks at a fixed width. I added text and photos to complete the page. A lot of empty space is to the right of the content, and

the navigation's graphic area ends abruptly (see Figure 36.1).

STEP 2: CREATE TILING BACKGROUND GRAPHIC FOR HEADER AREA

■ Using the existing layout, hide any layers sitting above the black and yellow pattern until all you see is the pattern. Using guides and the **Crop** tool, select one complete section of the pattern. See **Figure 36.4**. As soon as you are satisfied with the selection, double-click anywhere within the selected area to crop the image.

■ You now have only that small, cropped area on your screen. Choose **File ➢ Export** to export this image. You can find an example of this exported image, called header_background.gif, on the CD-ROM for reference.

> **NOTE**
>
> If you are not familiar with how to export a layout from Fireworks to HTML, see Technique 4 in Chapter 1.

36.3

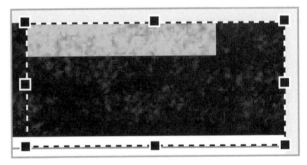

36.4

STEP 3: REBUILD EXPORTED HTML TABLES TO INCLUDE TILING BACKGROUND

■ In Dreamweaver, open the HTML file you exported from Fireworks (or ImageReady). Your goal here is to rebuild the navigation area so that the main table that holds it all together has this new tiling background graphic. See the file called Technique36_finished.htm on the CD-ROM for a finished example.

■ While in Design View, click the page to insert the cursor before any other content on the page. Insert a new table with five rows and one column.

■ Place your cursor in the first row of this new table and use the Property inspector to add the background image to that cell. Click the **Browse** button next to the BG field to browse for the tiling background graphic. Select it and click **OK**. See **Figure 36.5**.

■ Still in this cell, insert another table, this time with one row and three columns. In the first column, insert the title image (City Summer Camp). You can copy and paste this from the old table that should still be on your page. Repeat this step for the other two images in this row.

■ Next, create a 1 row/5 column table, and copy and paste the table containing the navigation into the second row of the new table. With the navigation table still selected, right-align the table by using the Property inspector.

■ In the third row of the new table, insert a horizontal rule (choose **Insert ➢ Horizontal Rule**). Change the appearance of the rule in the Property inspector. The width should be **100%**, Shading should be unchecked, and the height should be 1 pixel.

■ In the fourth row, copy and paste the content from your old table. This can remain the same; just make sure that if it's a nested table, that table is also set to a width of 100%.

36.5

■ Use the last row as a footer area. Give it a height of **20** pixels and a **black** background. Insert footer text, such as a copyright notice or an e-mail address.

■ Remove all traces of the fixed-width table below the new autostretch table, save, and preview in your browser. See **Figure 36.6**.

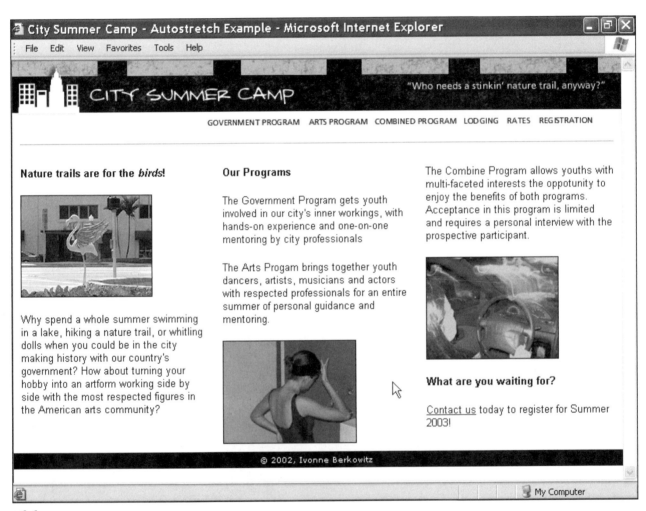

36.6

CHAPTER 8

TECHNIQUES TO SAVE YOU REPETITION

If you're working on a Web site, you probably don't have any time to waste, especially on boring, repetitive tasks. So you'll be pleased to discover that Dreamweaver really shines when it comes to features that automate tedious activities, such as changing one element of your navigation bar across every page on your site.

In the earliest days of the Web, if you wanted to change an element, such as a link that appeared on every page on your Web site, you had to manually change each instance individually. At the time, the best you could hope for was to automate the process with a program that had a good global search and replace feature, but even then it only worked if you had created every link exactly the same way on every page.

Today you have several ways to add elements to every page on your site and easily change all of them automatically if you want to make edits or additions later. One way is to use Dreamweaver's Library feature, which enables you to store any element or collection of elements, such as a logo or a navigation bar, in a way that makes it easy to add them to new pages and to make global changes. Technique 37 walks you through the steps to create and use Library items. Technique 38 shows you how to use frames to create navigation elements that can also be easily changed.

If you want to save time on formatting, Technique 39 shows you how to create HTML styles to automate formatting, and Technique 40 introduces you to the full power of Cascading Style Sheets. And finally, Technique 41 shows you how to save time by managing multimedia files with the Assets panel.

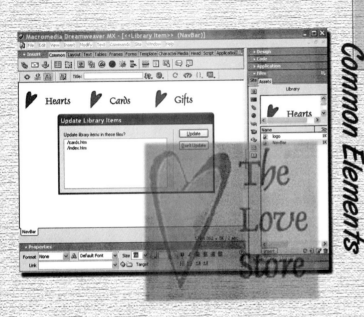

MULTIMEDIA ASSETS

Janine Warner
Communications

Automate
Formatting

In search of a simple computer

Cascading

FRAME NAVIGATION

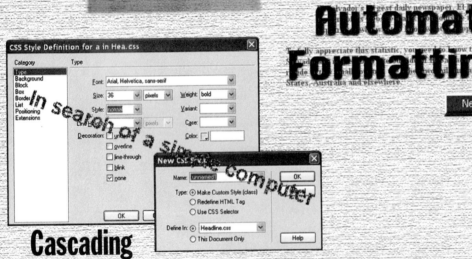

By Janine Warner

CREATING A LIBRARY OF COMMON ELEMENTS

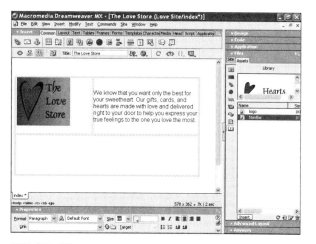

37.1 (CP 51)

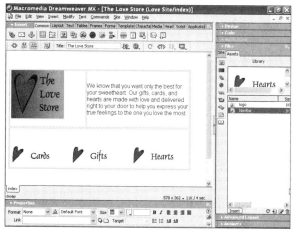

37.2 (CP 52)

L ibrary elements can save you time and tedium by providing an easy way to add commonly used items to multiple pages and to make global changes automatically.

The Library feature is not a common feature in other Web design programs, so the concept may be new to you, even if you've been developing Web sites for a while. The more experienced you are, however, the more likely you are to appreciate the value of this feature and the time it can save you.

The Dreamweaver Library feature was designed to automate the process of inserting and changing elements that appear on multiple pages in a Web site. You can save any element as a Library item — for example, a logo or a navigation row of images and links. You can then insert that element (or collection of elements) on any page by simply dragging it from the Library to the new page, which is what you see happening between **Figures 37.1 (CP 51)** and **37.2 (CP 52)**. Even better, if you ever need to change the Library element (by adding a link or image, for example), you can change the element in the Library and let Dreamweaver automatically apply the changes everywhere you've inserted the Library item in your site.

A *Library item* is essentially a snippet of code that can contain image references and links. Like templates, Library items are a great way to share the work of your best designers with less experienced ones. For example, a designer can create a logo and navigation elements, and then these items can be placed in the Library and made available to the rest of the team. And you have more flexibility with Library items than you do with Templates because you can place Library items anywhere on any page, even multiple times.

Library items can be made up of any element from the body of a document, including text, tables, forms, images, Java applets, and multimedia files. Library elements are efficient because Dreamweaver stores the snippet of code as a document in the Library folder and then updates the links to it from wherever the Library element is applied. Library items can also contain behaviors, but there are special requirements for editing the behaviors in Library items. Library items cannot contain timelines or style sheets.

STEP 1: CREATE A LIBRARY ITEM

The following sections lead you through the steps for creating a Library item, adding one to a page, and editing a Library item when an element changes. For these steps to work appropriately, you must do them carefully, in sequential order. Before creating or using Library items, you must first define a site or open an existing defined site.

To create a Library item that you can use on multiple pages on your site, follow these steps:

■ Open any existing file that has images, text, or other elements on the page or create a new file with any of these elements.

■ Select an element that you want to use as a Library item. A navigation row with images and links, such as the one selected in **Figure 37.3**, is an ideal use of the Library feature.

■ From the Files panel group, click the **Assets** tab and then click the last icon, the **Library** icon, shown in **Figure 37.4**.

■ Name the element as you would name any file in the Finder on a Mac or in Explorer on a PC. When you name a Library item, you automatically save it to the Library, so that you can then easily apply it to any new or existing page in your site. All Library items are listed in the Library section of the Assets panel, as shown in Figure 37.4.

STEP 2: ADD A LIBRARY ITEM TO A PAGE

You can take elements out of the Library as easily as you put them in. When you add a Library item to a page, the content (or a link to it) is inserted in the document, as well.

To add a Library item to a page, follow these steps:

■ Create a new document in Dreamweaver or open any existing file.

■ From the Files panel click the **Assets** tab and then click the **Library** icon. The Library panel opens in the Assets panel on the right side of the work area.

■ Drag an item from the Library panel to the document window, as shown in **Figure 37.5**. Alternatively, you can select an item in the Library panel and click the **Insert** button. The item automatically appears on the page. After you insert a

37.3

Library item on a page, you can use any of Dreamweaver's formatting features to position it on the page.

STEP 3: HIGHLIGHT LIBRARY ITEMS

Library items are highlighted to distinguish them from other elements on a page. You can customize the highlight color for Library items and show or hide the highlight color in Highlighting preferences.

To change or hide Library highlighting, follow these steps:

- Choose **Edit ➤ Preferences** and then **Highlighting** from the Category section on the left.

37.4

- Click the color box to select a color for Library items. Check the **Show** check box to display the Library highlight color on your pages. Leave the check box blank if you don't want to display the highlight color.
- For the Library highlight color to be visible in the document window, you must also be sure that the Show Library Items box is checked in the Highlighting section of the Preferences dialog box. Click **OK** to close the Preferences dialog box.

STEP 4: EDIT A LIBRARY ITEM TO MAKE GLOBAL CHANGES

One of the biggest timesaving advantages of the Dreamweaver Library feature is that you can make changes to items and automatically apply those changes to multiple pages. First, you edit the original Library item file; then you can choose to update the edited item in any one or all the documents in the current site.

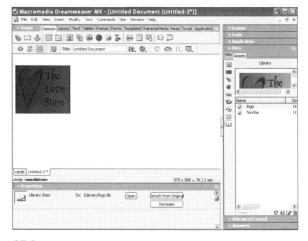

37.5

To edit a Library item and then update one or all of the pages on which you use that item, follow these steps:

- If it's not already open, click to open the Assets panel in the Files panel and click the **Library** icon.
- Select the item you want to alter by double-clicking its name in the Library panel to open it. Dreamweaver opens the Library item in the main work area where you can use Dreamweaver's standard editing functions to make any changes you want to the Library item. For example, you can change a link, alter text, insert or remove images, or change formatting.
- After you make all of the changes you want, choose **File ➢ Save** to save changes to the original item or choose **File ➢ Save As** and give it a new name to create a new Library item.
- If you choose **File ➢ Save**, the Update Library items dialog box opens, displaying a list of all pages where the Library item appears and prompting you to update all pages where the Library item is inserted (see **Figure 37.6**).

- Choose **Update** to apply your changes to all of the pages where your Library item is already inserted. Choose **Don't Update** to save your changes to the Library item without applying those changes to pages where the item has already been inserted.

STEP 5: MAKE LIBRARY ITEMS EDITABLE

If you decide that you want to alter a Library item in just one place or make just a couple of exceptions, you can override the Library feature by breaking the link between the Library and the item in the document and then editing the item as a static element on the page where it has been applied.

WARNING

Remember that after you break the connection, you cannot update the Library item automatically.

WARNING

Because Library items can contain only Body elements, but no Body attributes, the Style panel, the Timeline, and Page Properties are unavailable when you are editing a Library item. The Behaviors panel is also unavailable because it inserts code into the Head as well as the Body.

Update Library Items

Update library items in these files?
/cards.htm
/index.htm

Update
Don't Update

37.6

To make a Library item editable, follow these steps:

■ Open any file that contains a Library item and click to select the Library item. The Property inspector changes to display the Library item options.

■ Click the **Detach from Original** button to break the link from the Library. A warning message appears, letting you know that if you proceed with detaching the Library item from the original, it will no longer be possible to update this occurrence of it when the original is edited.

■ Click **OK** to detach the Library item. After a Library item is detached, it appears on the page as any other element. For example, if the Library item is an image, when you break the link to the Library, the image becomes a static image on the page, just as if you had inserted it directly on the page. If the image is linked to another page, the link to the page remains intact when the link to the Library is severed.

CREATING EFFECTIVE FRAME NAVIGATION

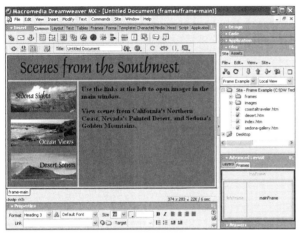

38.1 (CP 53)

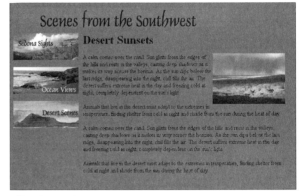

38.2 (CP 54)

NOTE

You can find all of the files used in this technique in the folder called Technique 38 on the CD-ROM.

Frames serve multiple purposes, but what's unique about them is that they enable you to display multiple HTML pages in one browser window and control the contents of each page, displayed in separate frames, individually. Designers commonly use frames to create a page with two or more sections and then place links in one section that, when selected, display information in another section of the same browser window.

Figures 38.1 (CP 53) and **38.2 (CP 54)** demonstrate how one navigation frame, in this case the frame on the left, can be used to display different content in another frame, in this case the frame on the right. Figure 38.1 (CP 53) shows the frame being built in Dreamweaver; Figure 38.2 (CP 54) shows the frameset displayed in Internet Explorer with the Desert Link selected.

Frames can save you time because navigation elements are stored on only one page, instead of being inserted on multiple pages. Thus, if you need to change the nav bar later, you only have to change one page to fix it throughout the site. The same goes for the frame at the top that holds the banner for this site. If I want to change that, I only have to change one page and the banner will display correctly with every other page on the site.

Web pages that use frames are split into separate sections—or individual *frames*. All the frames together make up a *frameset*. Behind the scenes, each frame of the frameset is a separate HTML file, which makes a page with frames a little complicated to create, even with Dreamweaver.

STEP 1: CREATE A FRAME BY USING THE FRAMES INSERT PANEL

The easiest way to create frames in Dreamweaver is with the Frames Insert panel, as shown in **Figure 38.3**. The Frames Insert panel (available by selecting the **Frames** tab from the Insert panel at the top of the work area) displays several predefined frames icons. You can create a frameset in Dreamweaver simply by clicking any of these icons or by dragging and dropping the icon into your document when you are in Design View. **Figure 38.4** shows a new frameset created from the Top and Nested Left Frames icon in the Frames Insert panel.

To create a framed page by using the icons in the Frames panel, follow these steps.

■ Choose **File** ➢ **New** ➢ **HTML Page** to create a new page.

■ From the Frames Insert panel, click the frames icon that most closely approximates the type of frameset you want to build and drag it onto your page in Design View. Click the icon once to apply it; I chose the Top and Nested Left Frames icon. Don't worry if you can't find exactly the design you want: You can alter the frameset after it's applied.

■ Modify the frameset as needed. Change the size of each frame by clicking and dragging the border. You can also add more frames by splitting existing frames. To split a frame, click to select the frame you want to split and choose **Modify** ➢ **Frames**. Then, select from the list of options to split the frame Left, Right, Top, Bottom, or any of several Nested options. You can also drag additional

38.3

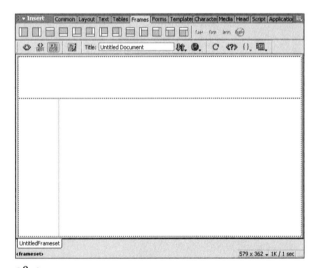

38.4

frame icons from the Frames panel into existing frames to divide them with predefined framesets.

■ To save your files, continue with Step 2.

STEP 2: SAVE FILES IN A FRAMESET

You shouldn't save a frameset until *after* you create all of the frames; otherwise, keeping track of your files gets very complicated. Remember, frames in HTML consist of at least two or more HTML files, even if it appears as if you are only working on one file. You have the frameset file, which calls the other frames into place, and a separate file for each frame area.

When you are ready to save, Dreamweaver gives you multiple save options for saving all the files. You can either save everything all at once by choosing **File ➢ Save All**, or you can save each frame and frameset individually, by clicking in each frame and choosing **File ➢ Save Frame**. To save the frameset document separately, use the Frames panel in the Advanced Layout panel (shown in **Figure 38.5**) to the right of the work area.

In the example in Step 1, I created four separate HTML files, three for the frame areas and one for the frameset. To save all the files in any frames document, follow these steps.

■ Choose **File ➢ Save All**. In the Save As dialog box, enter a name for the frameset (the first document to be saved) and designate a folder in which to save it. As soon as you name and save the frameset file, you will be prompted to save the first of the frames documents.

■ Enter a name for each file (or just click **Save** to accept the automatic name Dreamweaver recommends, which is something like Untitled-1, Untitled-2, and so forth.). You are prompted to name every frame in the frameset. The frame that you are naming is highlighted in the document window while the Save As dialog is open so you can see which frame you are naming.

■ After you name the last of the files, the dialog box closes when you click **Save**.

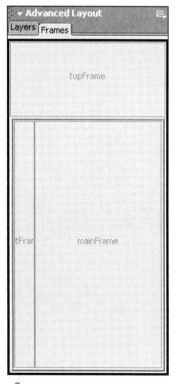

38.5

> **REMINDER**
>
> Naming the *frame* is different from naming the *file* that the frame represents; the *frame name* is like a nickname that allows you to distinguish your frames from one another on a page and refer to them individually. The *filename* is the actual name of the HTML file for the frame. (If you've ever created an image rollover, you had to give each image a name so you could distinguish them. Naming frames is very similar.)

STEP 3: NAMING FRAMES

Before you can set links within a frameset, you need to do a few things. First, you need to *name* each frame so that you can specify where the linked file should load. By that, I don't mean you need to name the file itself — you just did that when you saved the files. When you *name* a frame, you give the frame an identifier, which is part of the document code of the frameset. This *name*, or identifier, is then used to target the frame area when you set links.

To specify the names of the frames in your frameset, follow these steps.

- Create a new frameset or open an existing one and make sure that you save all the files.
- Choose **Window ➤ Others ➤ Frames** to open the Frames panel at the right of the work area. The Frames panel is a miniature representation of the frames on your page that enables you to select different frames by clicking within the panel, as shown in **Figure 38.6**.
- Click to place your cursor in the area of the Frames panel that corresponds to the frame that you want to name. In Figure 38.6, you can see that I selected the top frame, which is called topFrame. You can also select the entire frameset by clicking the border around all the frames in the Frames panel window, but you don't need to name the frameset. The Frames panel allows you to select only one frame or frameset at a time.

> **REMINDER**
>
> You can name your frame files anything you want, but you need a distinct name for each frame. I like to give names, such as frame1.html, frame2.html, or leftframe.html, rightframe.html so that it's easier to identify them later. It doesn't matter, but it is helpful if you use names that help you distinguish them. After you save all the frames, the Save dialog box disappears.

- When you select any frame area, the Property inspector changes to display the properties for that frame, making it possible for you to alter any of the frame's properties. In the text box on the

> **REMINDER**
>
> Dreamweaver assigns names automatically when you save the files in a frameset. In the example shown in Figure 38.6, Dreamweaver assigned the names topFrame, mainFrame, and leftFrame. You can leave these names as is or change them to something else in the Property inspector. I recommend naming frames with descriptive words, such as Nav-Frame, Banner-Frame, or Content-Frame, so that you can easily tell which frame is which by its name.

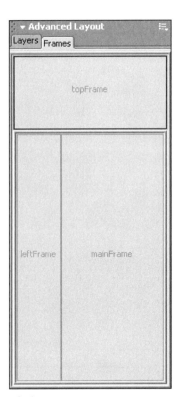

38.6

left side of the Property inspector, you should see the same name as appears in the Frames panel, which Dreamweaver has already automatically named. You can keep this name or enter a new name, which is what I'm doing in **Figure 38.7**. What's most important is that you know what each frame area is called so that you can recognize it in the target field when you set links within your frameset, as you see in Step 4.

■ Save each file after changing its name. You can either save each frame individually or choose the **Save All** command. Refer to Step 2, earlier in this technique, for more information on saving frames.

Now that you identified or changed the names of your frames, you're ready to start setting links that

target frames. Don't close these files yet — you want to use them to follow the next step, setting links.

STEP 4: SET TARGETS AND LINKS IN FRAMES

One of the best features of frames is that you can change the contents of each frame separately within the Web browser. This feature opens a wide range of design possibilities that can improve navigation for your site. One of the most common is to use a frame to keep a navigation bar constantly visible and open the page each navigation item links to in a separate frame area.

Setting links in a frameset requires some preliminary work. If you jumped to this section without having created a frameset or naming your frames, you may want to refer to the earlier steps that walk you through the process of saving and naming your frames. If you already have a frameset, have named the frames, and just want find out how to set links, this is where you want to be.

Links in a frameset work much like links anywhere else, except that in addition to indicating which page you want to open with the link, you have to specify which frame section it should *target* (or open into). For example, if you want a link in the left frame to display in the main frame, such as the example shown in this technique, you need to specify the main frame as the target in the link. If you don't specify a target, the link opens in the same frame in which the link is. Because the most common reason to use frames is to

38.7

keep navigation links in one frame and open them in another, you probably want to know how to target a frame when you set a link.

If this seems confusing, don't fret. Understanding it is easier after you try doing it. Follow these steps to create a targeted link in a frameset.

- Click to select an image or highlight text that you want to serve as the link. In the example shown in **Figure 38.8**, I selected the top image in the left frame.

- In the Property inspector, click the **Browse** button (the one that looks like a small file folder) next to the Link box. Browse to find the file to which you want to link. If you're using the sample files, you want to link this image to the Sedonagallery.htm file. Click the filename to select the file and choose **OK**, just like you would to set any other link to a file in your Web site.

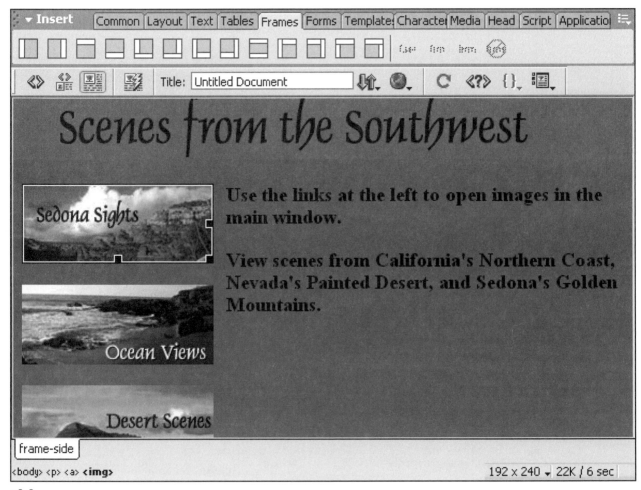

38.8

■ If it's not already expanded, make sure that the Property inspector is open to reveal the advanced options. (Use the small arrow in the bottom-right corner to expand the Property inspector.)

■ From the drop-down list next to Target in the bottom half of the Property inspector, choose the name of the frame into which you want the link to open. See **Figure 38.9**.

■ If you are following this exercise with the files on the CD-ROM, select mainFrame. If you changed the names, choose the name that corresponds to the frame you want the link to open into on the page. Notice that Dreamweaver conveniently lists all the frames you named in your document in this drop-down list.

■ To create additional links, repeat these steps. Essentially, what you are doing is creating a link

as you would create any other link, except that you are specifying the Target, meaning the area in the frameset where the linked page will open.

See **Figure 38.10** for the finished Web site.

REMINDER

You have to save your work before you preview it in a browser to test the link and ensure that you have properly targeted the frame. Press **F12** as a shortcut to Save All Files and open them in a browser automatically.

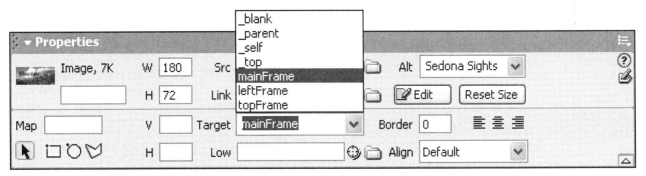

38.9

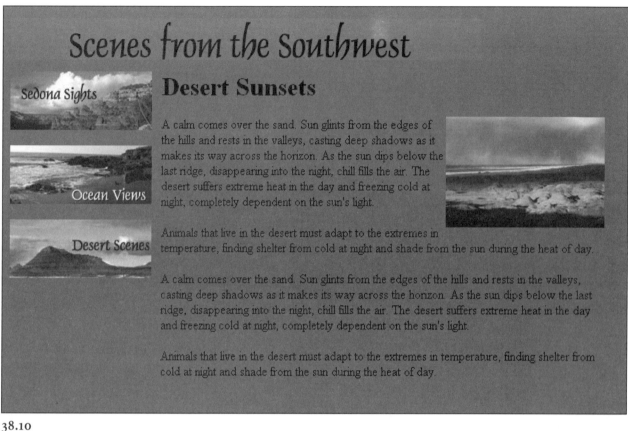

Scenes from the Southwest

Desert Sunsets

A calm comes over the sand. Sun glints from the edges of the hills and rests in the valleys, casting deep shadows as it makes its way across the horizon. As the sun dips below the last ridge, disappearing into the night, chill fills the air. The desert suffers extreme heat in the day and freezing cold at night, completely dependent on the sun's light.

Animals that live in the desert must adapt to the extremes in temperature, finding shelter from cold at night and shade from the sun during the heat of day.

A calm comes over the sand. Sun glints from the edges of the hills and rests in the valleys, casting deep shadows as it makes its way across the horizon. As the sun dips below the last ridge, disappearing into the night, chill fills the air. The desert suffers extreme heat in the day and freezing cold at night, completely dependent on the sun's light.

Animals that live in the desert must adapt to the extremes in temperature, finding shelter from cold at night and shade from the sun during the heat of day.

38.10

USING HTML STYLES TO AUTOMATE FORMATTING

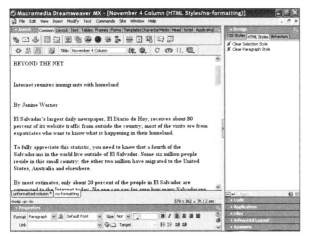

39.1 (CP 55)

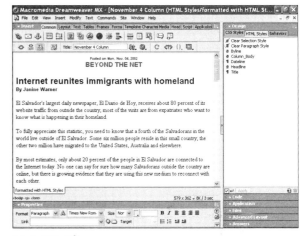

39.2 (CP 56)

If you want to save some time, you can save commonly used formatting attributes as a style that can be applied over and over again.

Don't confuse HTML styles with Cascading Style Sheets (covered in the next technique). HTML styles are simply a collection of <FONT> tags and other style attributes that you can save in Dreamweaver and then easily reuse.

HTML styles are convenient and very easy to create, but they are more limited than Cascading Style Sheets. First of all, they only let you apply font attributes that are available as part of regular HTML. This means that you can't specify font sizes based on pixels, picas, or any other measurement other than the normal, very limited, HTML sizes. HTML styles also can't be shared among sites unless the other sites are also being edited in Dreamweaver. No other HTML program can use or modify Dreamweaver HTML styles.

Perhaps the greatest limitation of HTML styles compared with Cascading Style Sheets, however, is that if you format text to a certain style and later

185

change the style definition, the text you formatted earlier doesn't update automatically to reflect the changes to the style. Still, in many cases, HTML styles can save time if you find yourself applying the same style attributes over and over again, such as in **Figures 39.1 (CP 55)** and **39.2 (CP 56)**, where you see one of my columns with no formatting, and then another version with formatting. To make it easier to format my newspaper column, which I add to my own Web site regularly, I created HTML styles to format the body, headline, byline, and dateline more easily.

STEP 1: CREATE AN HTML STYLE

Here's an example of how you can use HTML styles. Say you want all the headlines on your site to be font face Arial, size 5, and bold. You can create a style called Headline and apply all of those formatting options at once when you use the Headline style. If you want different size headlines, you can create a style sheet that defines Headline 1 as one size and Headline 2 as a smaller size for sub heads.

To create a new HTML style, follow these steps:

- Choose **Window ➤ HTML Styles** to open the HTML Styles panel in the Design panel to the right of the Dreamweaver work area.
- Open the panel Options drop-down menu by clicking the Options icon in the top-right corner of the panel group. (The Options icon looks like three very small bulleted items with a little arrow at the bottom of it.) Choose **New** from the pull-down list shown in **Figure 39.3**.
- Alternatively, you can choose **Text ➤ HTML Styles ➤ New Style** and then choose **New** from the submenu.

- Either one of the previous options opens the Define HTML Style dialog box shown in **Figure 39.4**.
- Enter a name in the text box at the top of the Define HTML Style dialog box. You can name the style anything you want. In the example shown in Figure 39.4, I chose to name a style **Headline**. The name you enter appears in the style menu after you create the style and is used only to identify the style.
- Specify if the style should be applied only to selected text elements or to all elements separated

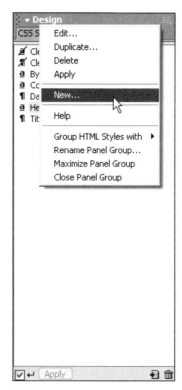

39.3

by the paragraph tag. Be aware that you have more control over which elements you apply the style to if you choose **Selection** instead of **Paragraph**.

■ Specify the behavior of the style when it is applied. If you want the style you create to be applied in addition to existing formatting, choose **Add to Existing Style** (+). If you want to clear any existing formatting before applying the new style, choose **Clear Existing Style**.

■ Select all formatting attributes, including Font, Size, Color, Style, and Alignment, that you want to include in this style. The Paragraph attributes are

only available if you have selected **Paragraph** in the Apply To section at the top of the dialog box.

■ Click **OK** to save the style. The new style automatically appears in the HTML Styles panel and becomes available in the submenu when you choose **Text ➤ HTML Styles**. The HTML Style you created remains as an option in the HTML Styles menu until you remove it.

STEP 2: APPLY AN HTML STYLE

As soon as you create a new style, you can apply it to any string of text. To apply an existing HTML style, follow these steps.

■ Highlight the text you want to modify and choose **Text ➤ HTML Styles**.

■ Click to select one of the styles from the Styles submenu, and the style is automatically applied to your selected text. The Styles submenu features all of the predefined styles that ship with Dreamweaver, as well any custom styles you create.

■ Alternatively, you can apply a style to a selected area of text by highlighting the text and clicking a style name in the HTML Styles panel in the Design panel to the right of the Dreamweaver work area.

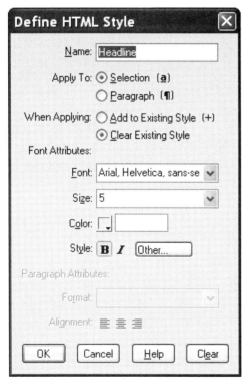

39.4

> **REMINDER**
>
> HTML styles are stored on your hard drive in a file called styles.xml. This folder is located either in the site folder (in the Library subfolder) or in the Dreamweaver configuration folder if the site root folder has not been defined.

LET CASCADING STYLE SHEETS GUIDE YOUR WORK

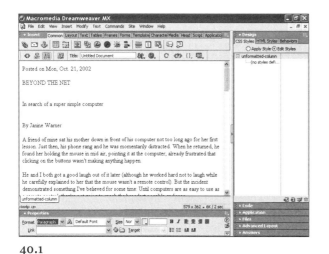

40.1

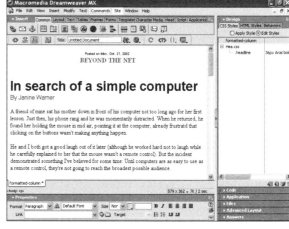

40.2

NOTE

You can find all of the files used in this technique in the folder called Technique 40 on the CD-ROM.

E ven if you're not familiar with the concept of style sheets, you're sure to appreciate the benefits. Cascading Style Sheets, more commonly referred to by the acronym *CSS*, enable you to define styles with multiple text formatting options in HTML. CSS goes a long way toward giving you real typographic control and a consistent look and feel throughout a Web site, as well as saving time in designing your Web page.

One of the greatest advantages of CSS styles is that you can create external style sheets, which means that one style sheet can be applied to multiple pages, such as the ones I used to format the different text areas in my column, shown in **Figure 40.1** before applying styles, and **Figure 40.2** after applying styles.

Before you get too excited, however, I have to warn you that because CSS is a relatively new addition to HTML, the more advanced formatting options may not display consistently in all browsers. If you want to play it safe, use the most basic CSS options or stick with HTML styles, featured in Technique 39.

STEP 1: CREATE AN EXTERNAL CSS STYLE

The greatest advantage to using CSS to format my column instead of HTML styles is that I can create one external style sheet and use it to format all of my columns, just as I did with the one in Figure 40.2. The following steps show you how to use Dreamweaver to create an external style sheet. In this example, you define a style for headlines by using CSS. If you want to create a style for another element, follow these same steps but change the specific attributes.

You can leave attributes unspecified if you don't want to use them. If you don't specify them, the browser uses its own defaults. For example, I don't recommend using any of the Decoration options because they can distract and confuse viewers.

To define an external style sheet for all your headlines, follow these steps.

■ Choose **Text ➢ CSS Styles ➢ New CSS Style** to open the New CSS Style dialog box, shown in **Figure 40.3**. The new style is automatically called .unnamed1.

■ In the Name text box, type a new name for the style. Dreamweaver gives you a default name that begins with a period (.) because these types of style names must begin with a period. You can

name the style anything you want as long as you don't use spaces or punctuation. Dreamweaver adds the initial period to the class name even if you omit it.

■ Next to Type select **Make Custom Style (class)**.

■ Next to Define In, select an existing style sheet (as shown in Figure 40.3) or create a new one by selecting New Style Sheet File. Either way, make sure that the radio button next to This Document Only is not selected. Click **OK** and the Save Style Sheet File As dialog box opens. Browse to the folder where you want to save the style, name the file in which the style sheet will be stored, and then click **Save**.

■ In the CSS Style Definition dialog box, choose a font or font set from the Font drop-down list. If you want to use fonts that aren't on the list, choose **Edit Font List** from the drop-down list to create new font options.

■ From the Size drop-down list, choose the size you want for your headline. Large headlines are generally 24 or 36 point. You may prefer to choose a relative size, such as large or larger.

■ From the Style drop-down list, choose a style. Italic and Oblique are both good for making text stand out on a page.

■ From the Weight drop-down list, choose **Bold** to make your headline thicker and darker.

40.3

> **NOTE**
>
> You can also add new styles to an existing style sheet. Click the Attach Style Sheet button at the bottom of the CSS Styles panel and follow the steps.

■ Ignore Variant and Case because these attributes aren't well supported by current browsers.

■ Click the Color box and choose a color from the color well. Sticking to the default color swatches in the color well is best because it ensures that you use a Web-safe color. You can also create a custom color by clicking the icon that looks like a rainbow-colored globe in the upper-right corner of the color well.

■ Click **OK** and your style is automatically added to the Styles list and the CSS Styles panel.

You can apply styles in the Styles list to any Web page or selected text block. After you create your style, it appears in the submenu under **Text ➤ CSS Styles**. Any text that you apply it to takes on the formatting attributes you just specified. For more on how to use styles, see Step 3, "Apply Styles," later in this technique.

STEP 2: REDEFINE AN HTML TAG TO ELIMINATE UNDERLINE FROM LINKS

When you create a custom style as you did in the previous step, you start a completely new style with its own unique name. When you redefine an HTML tag, however, you begin with an existing HTML tag, such as <B> (bold), <HR> (horizontal rule), or <TABLE> (table), and change the attributes associated with that specific tag. Any new attributes that you apply through CSS to an existing tag override the existing attributes.

To redefine a tag, start a new CSS style by clicking the **New CSS Style** button at the bottom right of the panel and then selecting **Redefine HTML Tag** in the New CSS Style dialog box. When you choose this option, a list of tags appears at the top of the dialog box. Choose the tag that you want to change from the

Tag drop-down list shown in **Figure 40.4**. Then, define how you want to change it by altering the various categories and attributes in the CSS Style Definition dialog box. Be aware that when you redefine an existing HTML tag, any text that you've already formatted with that tag changes to reflect the new definition.

Now that you know how to redefine an HTML tag, here's your chance to put it into practice. One of the most commonly used HTML tag modifications involves disabling the underline for the anchor tag, <A>, so that hypertext links are no longer underlined

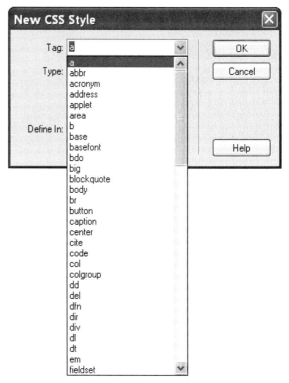

40.4

in the browser. Many Web designers like to remove the underline because they think it detracts from the design and also because the cursor changes to a hand over any link, making the underline unnecessary. This technique works in both Netscape and Internet Explorer 4.0 (and above) browsers.

To disable underlining for hypertext links, follow these steps.

■ Choose **Text ➤ CSS Styles ➤ New CSS Style** and then **Redefine HTML Tag**. From the Tag pull-down list, choose the anchor tag <**a**>.

■ Next to Define In, select **This Document Only** and click **OK** to open the CSS Style Definition dialog box, shown in **Figure 40.5**. (If you want the style to apply to the entire site, choose New Style Sheet File.)

■ Make sure that the **Type** category is selected, and then check the **none** check box under the Decoration section. Click **OK** to apply the changes.

After you click OK, active links are no longer under-lined on the page, even when displayed in a browser, as long as it's 4.0 or higher. In older browsers, the

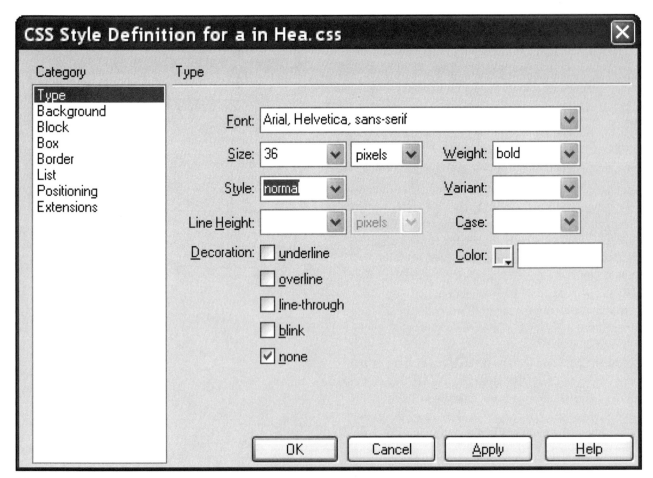

40.5

links appear with underlines, but otherwise are unaffected. You can make more modifications to the <a> tag in this manner, or you can apply the same principles to any of the other HTML tags available in the New CSS Style dialog box. Remember, any time you redefine an HTML tag by using CSS, the changes are visible in your page only if those tags are actually used.

STEP 3: APPLY STYLES

Defining styles is the complicated part. Applying them after you define them is easy. You simply select the text that you want to affect and choose the predefined style that you want to apply.

To apply a style, follow these steps:

- Highlight the text to which you want to apply a style.
- Select the style that you want to apply from the list that appears in the white area of the CSS Styles panel, as shown in **Figure 40.6**. The style is automatically applied to the selection.

REMINDER

If the Style panel is not visible, choose **Window** ➢ **CSS Styles** to open it.

- You can also apply a custom style by selecting the text that you want to change by choosing **Text** ➢ **CSS Styles** and choosing a style from the submenu.

See **Figure 40.7** for the formatted column.

40.6

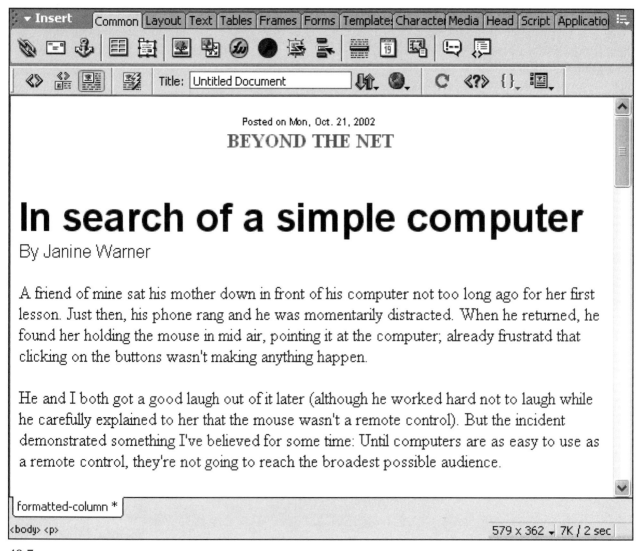

40.7

REUSING MULTIMEDIA ASSETS

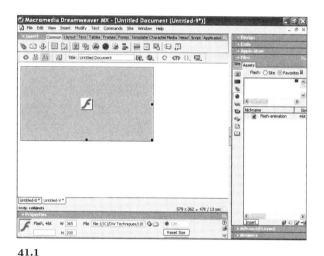

41.1

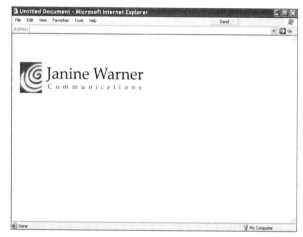

41.2

The Assets panel in Dreamweaver provides access to many timesaving features, including the multimedia assets panels where all of your multimedia files are automatically stored for easy access.

If you use a lot of multimedia elements in your Web site, such as sound files, animations, and video clips, you'll appreciate that the Assets panel automatically stores all of these elements as you add them to your pages so that you can easily add them to any of your pages. **Figure 41.1** shows a Flash file being added to a page from Dreamweaver's Assets panel, and **Figure 41.2** shows it being played in Internet Explorer.

STEP 1: SAVE FLASH ASSETS

As you add Flash files (movies, animations, and so on, created in Macromedia Flash), Dreamweaver automatically stores references to these files in the Flash Assets panel. To use the Flash Assets panel, follow these steps.

■ Click the **Assets** tab from the Files panel group in the panels that appear in the right of the Dreamweaver work area. Then, click the **Flash** icon at the top left of the Assets panel. The Flash files in your site appear in a list in the main area of the panel.

■ You can reorder Flash files by filename by clicking **Name**, by size by clicking **Size**, and by file type by clicking **Type**.

■ To insert a Flash file on a page, simply open the page in the main work area of Dreamweaver, click the filename in the Flash Assets panel, and drag it onto the page. Dreamweaver automatically inserts it on the page. You can then change the attributes of the Flash file in the Property inspector.

■ To add a Flash file to the Favorites section of the Flash Assets panel, right-click the filename and choose **Add to Favorites**, as shown in **Figure 41.3**. To view your Favorites, click the **Favorites** radio button at the top of the panel. The Favorites panel can help you if you have a lot of multimedia files and want to be able to more easily find the ones you use most frequently.

STEP 2: USING FLASH ASSETS

The Flash Assets panel stores all of your Flash files automatically. The advantage of this is that you can easily add Flash files to pages from the Assets panel. That means that if you want to use the same Flash file on multiple pages, you can insert it by simply dragging it from the Flash Assets panel to the new page.

To insert a Flash file from the Assets panel to a new page, follow these steps:

■ Click the **Assets** tab from the Files panel group in the panels that appear in the right of the Dreamweaver work area. Then, click the **Flash** icon, fourth down in the row at the left of the Assets panel. The Flash panel opens and all of the Flash files used in your site appear in a list in the main area of the Flash panel. (If all of your Flash files do not appear, try clicking the **Refresh** site icon at the bottom right of the panel. If they still don't appear, try restarting Dreamweaver.)

41.3

- To insert a Flash file on a page, create a new page or open an existing page in the main work area of Dreamweaver, click the name of the Flash file in the Assets panel, and drag it onto the page in the work area. Dreamweaver automatically inserts the Flash file on the page.

- To change the attributes of the Flash file, click to select the Flash file on the page and make your changes in the Property inspector. **Figure 41.4** shows the Flash Assets panel open, with the Flash file selected. The Property inspector displays the Flash attributes, as shown in **Figure 41.5**.

STEP 3: USING OTHER MULTIMEDIA ASSETS

In addition to Flash files, the Assets panel automatically stores Shockwave files, Movie files, and Scripts. All of these assets work the same way. When you add any of these multimedia assets to your pages, Dreamweaver automatically stores them in the corresponding assets panel.

If you want to add a multimedia asset to a new page, simply open the Assets panel, choose the Asset type by clicking the appropriate icon on the left side of the

panel, click to select the asset, and drag it onto the page. Dreamweaver automatically inserts the file on the page for you.

41.4

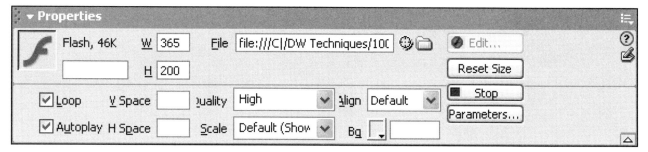

41.5

CHAPTER 9

DYNAMICALLY DISPLAY CONTENT WITH DATABASE FEATURES

Tired of editing individual pages every time you want to update your Web site? Is your site's content divided across so many unique pages that it would require weeks of labor to restructure your content into a new design? It sounds like you are in dire need of Dreamweaver's MX database features! The following techniques show you how you can separate your content from your Web pages to make your site easier to manage.

To complete the following techniques, you need to meet Dreamweaver's database prerequisites, such as defining your local site, installing IIS or the equivalent on a Macintosh, and creating DNS entries for your databases. The Databases panel in Dreamweaver includes all of the requirements needed to connect to a database. If you are new to setting up an application server, you'll find references at the end of this chapter to a couple of resources on the Web that can help you get started. You also find a more thorough explanation of dynamic site setup in *Dreamweaver MX For Dummies* and *Teach Yourself VISUALLY Dreamweaver MX*.

SCOURING YOUR DATABASE WITH AN EASY SITE SEARCH FEATURE

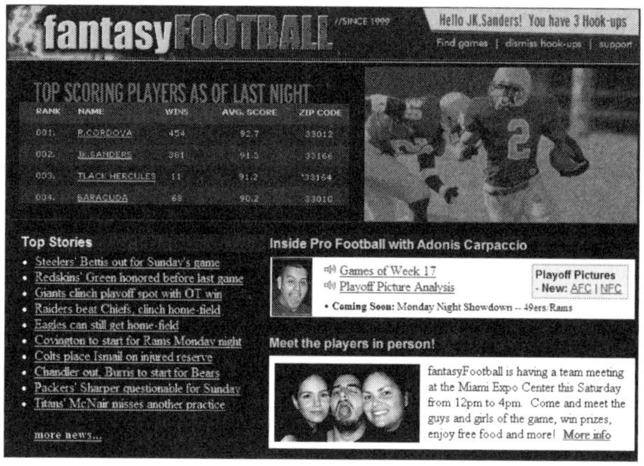

42.1 (CP 57)

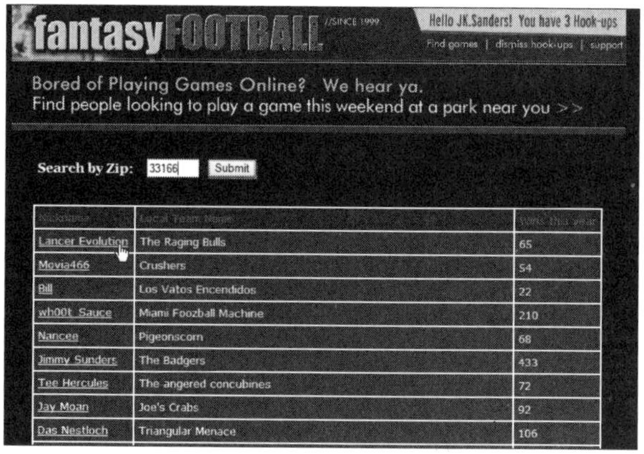

42.2 (CP 58)

> **NOTE**
>
> You can find the database used in this technique in the folder called Technique 42 on the CD-ROM. You should copy the MDB file to your computer and create a DSN entry for it using a Microsoft Access driver.

A site search enables people to query your database and view matching results through a Web browser. For example, **Figure 42.1 (CP 57)** shows how a fantasy football league Web site uses a database search to help its members. Their members simply enter their zip code, and the site dynamically displays information about other members in their area, as shown in **Figure 42.2 (CP 58)**.

STEP 1: CREATE A SEARCH FORM

The search form is the HTML component that sends the inputted request to the application server as a database query.

- Create and save a new ASP/VBScript page in your site folder.
- Choose **Insert ➢ Form**. A red dotted line appears, indicating the perimeter of the form.
- With your cursor inside the form perimeter, choose **Insert ➢ Form Objects ➢ Text Field**.

- Give your text field a name in the Property inspector, such as ZipField.
- Choose **Insert ➢ Form Objects ➢ Button**. A Submit button appears.

STEP 2: CREATE A RECORDSET

A *Recordset* is a collection of data retrieved from your database. **Figure 42.3** illustrates how you can create a specific query that narrows down the retrieved data for your Recordset. In this example, the Recordset is to be filtered by the Zip column.

- Open the Server Behaviors panel.
- Click the **Plus Sign** (+) button and choose **Recordset Query**. The Recordset dialog box appears, as shown in Figure 42.3. If this option is not available, follow the instructions in the Bindings panel on how to create a Connection.
- Enter a name for your Recordset. Dreamweaver rejects spaces and special characters, so enter a word or alphanumeric string.

- Choose your DSN connection from the pull-down menu. If you have not created a connection, you can define one by clicking the **Define** button.
- Choose the table from the database from which you'd like to select data columns. In this technique, you want to search the site's customer base, so select **Players**.
- Select the columns you want to display. You can either click the **All** radio button or click the **Selected** radio button and click individual column names in the menu below. Hold down the ⌘/Ctrl key to click more than one column if desired.
- Choose a filter by selecting a column name from the pull-down menu. In this technique, you are going to display matches of exact zip codes, so choose the **Zip** column and choose the = (**equal**) sign as the filter method.
- Change URL Parameter to **Form Variable** under the third filter menu.
- Enter the name of the form field you created in Step 1. In this example, the name is ZipField.
- Choose a sort method if desired (this is an optional step). You can sort your Recordset by column data by changing None to a column in

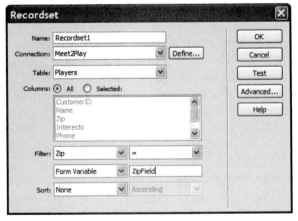

42.3

> **NOTE**
>
> You can't click the **Live Data** button in this technique to test your work because the application server requires data inputted into this form before it knows what data it needs to display. When you have completed the technique, you must test it with your Web browser.

this menu and choosing whether you want the results to appear in descending or ascending order.

■ Click **Test** to verify that the proper variables are set. Enter **33166** when prompted and click **OK**, as shown in **Figure 42.4**. The Test SQL window appears showing matching data. Close all testing windows and click **OK** to save your Recordset.

STEP 3: CREATE A SEARCH RESULTS ZONE

A Recordset is much like a variable in any application — its value remains unseen until you display it. The following steps demonstrate how you can

> **REMINDER**
>
> **If you cannot select the Recordset Query behavior after you have clicked the Plus Sign (+) button, you may not have set up your site correctly to handle a database connection. Make sure that IIS or PWS is installed *and* running, that your DNS is working, and that you selected the ASP/VBScript technology for your file type. Refer to this chapter's introduction for more information.**

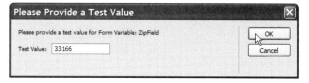

42.4

dynamically display the dynamic information residing in your Recordset. This example utilizes a three-column table to show the Name, Description, and Interests columns from the Recordset.

■ Create a multicolumn table outside of the form to house your Recordset by choosing **Insert** ➤ **Table** (**Ctrl+Alt+T**). You need only create one row: Additional rows are inserted dynamically by the application server's Repeat Region behavior.

■ Expand the Bindings panel and choose your Recordset. Click the small **Plus Sign** (+) button to reveal the columns in your Recordset.

■ Click and drag the desired columns from your Bindings panel directly into your table cells. A block of highlighted text with the column name appears on the page.

■ Select the Table tag from the Tag inspector at the bottom left of the document window to be sure the whole table is selected.

■ Expand the Server Behaviors panel and click the **Plus Sign** (+) button to reveal the available behaviors. Choose **Repeat Region**. The Repeat Region dialog box appears.

■ Choose the Recordset you want to display in the search results.

■ Choose how many search result (rows) you want to display or select the **All** option. Click **OK** to confirm this behavior.

■ With the table still selected, click the **Plus Sign** (+) button once more to add another behavior. This time choose the **Show Region** ➤ **If Recordset is NotEmpty** behavior.

■ Choose the Recordset you created for this page. Click **OK** to confirm your selection.

STEP 4: PREVIEW IN YOUR BROWSER

- Press **F12** on your keyboard or click the **Preview in Browser** icon on the Document Toolbar.
- Enter a search value into your form and click the **Submit** button. Search results appear in the repeat region if a match exists, as shown in **Figure 42.5**.

42.5

If your browser reports an HTTP 500 internal operation error or reports a similar OLE error about the database file being in use, save and close your document, close Dreamweaver, and navigate to it from `http://localhost`. You should also check to make sure your database isn't open within the Microsoft Access program, because that can also lock you out. You can decrease the chance of this happening by giving your IUSR account rights to the containing folder. Please refer to the end of this chapter and Appendix C for more information.

> **TIP**
>
> Showing all search results on one page can slow down your application and overwhelm your site visitors if your database contains a lot of content. Add pagination by specifying a limit in your Repeat Region behavior, and then add Recordset Paging behaviors or the Recordset Navigation object found in the Application Object submenu under the Insert menu.

INVITING INTERACTIVE GRAFFITTI INTO YOUR SITE WITH A PUBLIC GUEST BOOK

43.1

By acting as a digital bulletin board, a guest book is a quick and easy way to allow people visiting your Web site to post information. People fill out a form, and their entry is recorded into your database and displayed immediately by your server application. The online journal shown in **Figure 43.1** uses a guest book to allow visitors to discuss the latest post.

STEP 1: CREATE THE VIEW GUESTBOOK PAGE

The View Guestbook page displays the entries that have already been recorded in the database. Traditionally, this page is presented as the main guest book page, and the insert guest book page is linked from it. When creating your database for the guest book, include Fields Names, Contact Information, and Create One Comment columns.

■ Create and save a new ASP/VBScript page in your site folder.

■ Create a Recordset by clicking the Bindings panel **Plus Sign** (+) button and choosing **Recordset Query**. Create a connection for your Recordset if you have not already done so.

■ Choose your table and the desired columns you want to display from it. Make sure that your Primary Key is part of your Recordset. The Primary Key is the first column in the sample Access database that sequentially numbers all records.

■ Sort your Recordset by choosing **Descending** and then choose your Primary Key. If you are using the sample database, the Primary Key is the ID column. This step is optional but is recommended, because guest books usually show the most recent entry as the first. Click **OK** to save your Recordset.

■ Choose **Insert ➢ Application Objects ➢ Dynamic Table**. Choose your Recordset and click **OK** to close the Dynamic Table dialog box.

■ A table appears. Customize the rows and columns of the table to your liking. As shown in **Figure 43.2**, the designer set a third table row with merged cells to allow the person's comment to flow across the bottom of the contact information.

■ With the entire table selected, click the **Plus Sign** (+) button in the Server Behaviors panel and choose the **Show Region ➢ If Recordset is NotEmpty** behavior.

■ Choose the Recordset you created for this page. Click **OK** to confirm your selection.

■ Save and close this document. If you are having trouble previewing your document, please refer to Technique 42, Step 4.

STEP 2: CREATE THE INSERT ENTRY PAGE

The Insert Entry page inserts a row into your database with the information provided through a form on the Web browser. As soon as the person fills out the form and submits it, they are redirected to the View Guestbook page where they can see their entry appear immediately.

TIP

Some guest books give people the option to make their posts public or private. If you want to add this feature to your guest book, create a column in the database for a privacy value, which you can populate by adding a "private entry" check box on your insert form. You can then filter against this variable accordingly in your Recordset by using an argument such as CONTAINS or =.

43.2

- Create and save a new ASP/VBScript page in your site folder.
- Create the same Recordset you created on the View Guestbook page.
- Choose **Insert ➢ Application Objects ➢ Record Insertion Form**. The Insert Record dialog box appears (see **Figure 43.3**).

- Choose your connection, as you did in the previous steps.
- Choose the appropriate database table into which to insert new guest book entries.
- Click the **Browse** button and choose the ASP page you created for the View Guestbook page.
- If your Recordset has an autonumber ID, remove it by clicking that column name and then clicking the **Minus Sign** (–) button.
- Click **OK** to insert your record submission form.
- A table with a form tag and form elements appears on your page. Change the Insert Record label to something more relevant, such as "Post Message." Your form should appear similar to the table shown in **Figure 43.4**.

STEP 3: PREVIEW IN YOUR BROWSER

- Press **F12** on your keyboard or click the **Preview in Browser** icon on the Document Toolbar.
- Fill out the fields and press the **Submit** button to create a guest book entry, as shown in **Figure 43.5**.

43.3

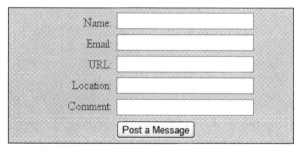

43.4

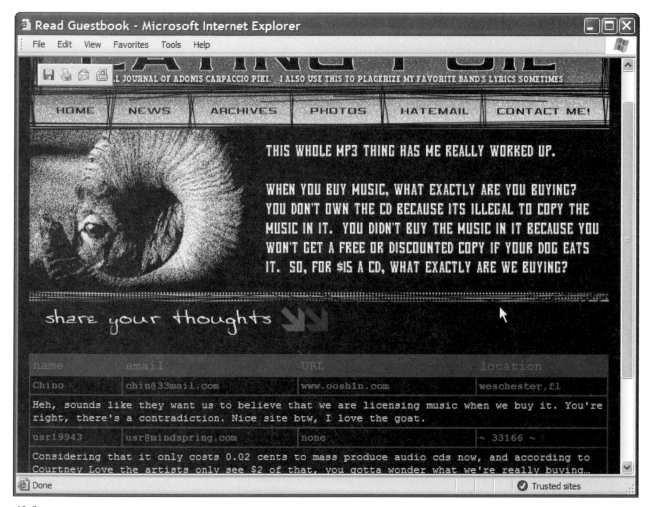

43.5

SHOWING OFF A PRODUCT CATALOG WITH A MASTER/DETAIL PAGE SET

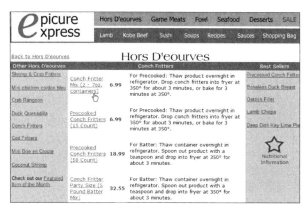

44.1 (CP 59)

44.2 (CP 60)

NOTE

You can find the database used in this technique in the folder called Technique 44 on the CD-ROM. You should copy the database to your computer, create a DSN, and set up a Connection within Dreamweaver before beginning this technique.

The most widely used method of presenting a group of similar items found in a database is to show a list of links with each item's link pointing to a page containing more information about the item. The list page, shown in **Figure 44.1 (CP 59)**, is often referred to as the Master page, and the page with the detailed information is known as the Detail page, shown in **Figure 44.2 (CP 60)**. The great thing about creating this dynamic duo is that you need to create only two ASP pages, regardless of how many thousand products are in a database. The two pages act as templates — only the body content changes, which allows you great flexibility in terms of site growth. It also means you don't have to convert hundreds of pages when you decide you want to refresh your site's graphics.

STEP 1: CREATE YOUR MASTER/ DETAIL SET

This Application object is different than the previous one you dealt with because it inserts server behaviors across two pages in one fell swoop. Because of this, you need to create both pages before the object command is initiated.

- Create a new ASP/VBScript page in your site folder.
- Save this document by choosing **File ➢ Save** (**Ctrl+S**).
- Name this file Detail.asp (or another descriptive name of your choice).
- Close this document, which you intentionally left blank. You return to it in Step 2.
- Create a new ASP/VBScript page in your site folder.
- Save this document by choosing **File ➢ Save** (**Ctrl+S**).
- Name this file Master.asp (or another descriptive name of your choice).

TIP

Technically speaking, you can make the Detail page behaviors and the Master page behaviors exist on the same document. I've found that this is not common practice, perhaps because of flexibility and manageability. If you want to experiment with this method, ignore the first few instructions in Step 1 and select the same document with the **Browse** button instead of choosing your Detail page.

STEP 2: APPLY THE MASTER/DETAIL OBJECT

Dreamweaver inserts everything you need to view the database content and navigate around the site as soon as you complete this step. The only work you have left to do is customization of the otherwise generic default layout of the object. You want your Master to be quick and easy to read, so only choose the most important columns on that page, shown in **Figure 44.3**.

- Create a Recordset containing the data you want to use.
- With your Master page open, choose **Insert ➢ Application Objects ➢ Master/Detail Page Set**. A dialog box appears, as shown in **Figure 44.4**.
- Select the appropriate Recordset from the drop-down menu.
- Use the **Minus Sign** (–) button to remove any fields you don't want shown in your Master page. If you accidentally remove one you want to keep or want to add more, click the **Plus Sign** (+) button.
- The Link To Detail From menu places a hyperlink around the database column of your choice. Choose a column that best summarizes the item, such as its name. If you are using the sample database, choose **ITEM_NAME**.

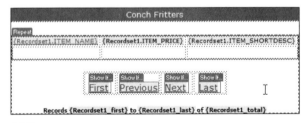

44.3

- Select your Primary Key in the Pass Unique Key menu. The sample database's Primary Key is **SKU**.
- Select the number of records you want to display on the Master screen. If you choose **All**, no navigation is added. If you enter a number instead, navigation links automatically appear at the bottom of the page that manages the pagination.
- Click the **Browse** button and choose the Detail.ASP page that you created in Step 1.
- Choose the columns you want to display in the Details page. You can manage what columns are inserted in the same way you specified the Master records.

- Click **OK** to close the dialog box. This executes the object, which inserts various server behaviors into your Master page, opens your Details page, adds server behaviors to it, and leaves the page open for further modification.
- Choose **File ➤ Save All** to save the changes you made to both Web pages. See **Figure 44.5** for the Detail Web page.

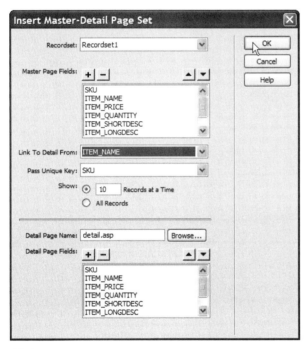

44.4

DYNAMIC IMAGES

To display images dynamically from a database, create a column in the database where you can write out the directory path (URL) of the image. Then, insert an image placeholder from the Insert menu and drag the lightning bolt icon from a Recordset column name to it. The placeholder transforms into a dynamic image icon, as shown below.

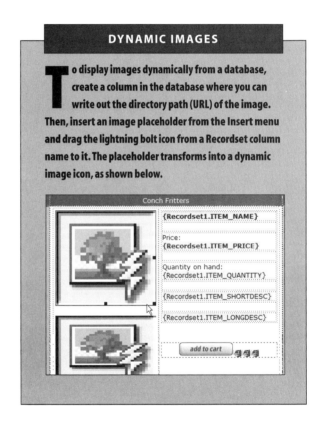

44.5

ADMINISTRATING YOUR DATABASE WITH YOUR WEB BROWSER

45.1

After creating your database structure, you can close Access for good and create specialized administrative Web pages to better manage your site. For example, you can isolate the management of product inventory, price, and descriptions for your product's database table. **Figure 45.1** shows how EpicureXpress uses a page to edit a product description without needing to view all products at once, or digging into any HTML code or database work. Their site also utilizes separate admin pages for managing customer data, zip code shipping rates, e-coupons, and sales reports that work in a similar manner. Setting up pages such as this also gives them the added benefit of being able to administrate their system from any Internet-connected computer.

STEP 1: CREATE THE RECORD UPDATE FORM

The Update Record object automatically inserts virtually every feature you need to manage any given row in a database. The components of the object include a form, text fields that pre-populate with the database content the row contains, and a Submit button that saves the changes you make.

■ Create and save a new ASP/VBScript page in your site folder.

■ Create a connection for your Recordset if you have not already done so in preparation.

■ Create a Recordset by clicking the Bindings panel **Plus Sign (+)** button and choosing **Recordset (Query)**. The Recordset dialog box appears. Choose any and all columns you want to administer with this form. Also include your Primary Key, even if it is an exclusive autonumber column. You use the Primary Key in a later step.

■ Choose **Insert ➢ Application Objects ➢ Record Update Form**. The Record Update Form dialog box appears.

■ Choose your connection and desired database table.

■ Choose the table you want to update from the **Select Table To Update** menu.

■ Choose the Recordset you created previously on the **Select Record From** menu.

■ Choose your Primary Key in the Unique Key Column menu. Specify whether or not it is numeric by checking the Numeric check box.

> **NOTE**
>
> You can't enter this string in the Record Update form screen. Dreamweaver won't understand that you are entering a dynamic variable and will move the quote marks around.

■ You may leave the Go To field blank: It's optional. If you want to stay on the admin page when you update the forms, leave it empty. If you prefer to see the page you just edited, choose your Detail page for the moment. When you have completed your selections in this dialog box, switch to Code View and find the variable called MM_editRedirectURL. Change its value to read:

```
MM_editRedirectUrl =
"detail.asp?SKU=" +
Request.Form("MM_recordId")
```

■ Choose the columns you want to display from your table. Remove your Primary Key column from this selection by clicking it and pressing the **Minus Sign (–)** button.

■ Use the Column menu at the bottom of the dialog box to individually set the data type submitted by the form. The most common is text, which allows for alphanumeric data.

> **TIP**
>
> Don't just rely on "security through obscurity" to safeguard your database — saving your administrative pages in an undisclosed location on your server does not protect you against all malicious activity. For starters, your administrative pages should be in a password-protected directory. Dreamweaver provides a user authentication server behavior you can use, or you can set a password on the folder within IIS. If you intend on storing sensitive information in your database, you should consider installing a firewall and a separate database server from the outside world, and then limiting port access to a trusted IP range and your Web server. If you are doing any kind of e-commerce, you should also look into adding encryption.

■ Click **OK** to generate the Update Record object. A form containing a table with dynamic data fields appears on your page.

STEP 2: CREATE RECORD NAVIGATION

Your Update Record form is programmed by default to look at the first entry in your Recordset. This means to edit another record, you either have to change your query or, better yet, create a navigation system that allows you to browse database content. By pairing up another Application object to the same page, you can achieve this goal.

■ Place your cursor inside of the Record Update form and press **Return/Enter** key to insert space between the existing table and the new table you are about to create.

■ Choose **Insert ➤ Application Objects ➤ Recordset Navigation Bar**. The Recordset Navigation Bar dialog box appears.

■ Choose the Recordset you selected in the Record Update Form dialog box.

TIP

If you are dealing with a large set of rows in your database, consider creating a more intuitive navigational menu. By combining a database search (refer to Technique 42) with the behaviors used in this object, you can locate records more efficiently. You can also include the Recordset Navigation Status object from the Application Object menu to show you how many total records are found in a query.

■ Choose whether you prefer text links or if you want Dreamweaver to generate image buttons for you. If you choose **image**, four green navigation buttons reminiscent of a tape deck appear; **text** produces four text links. Either choice provides the same functionality: the ability to move back and forth among records and jump to the first or last record.

■ Click **OK** to include the Recordset Navigation bar. It appears below your Record Update form, as shown in **Figure 45.2**.

TIP

Wondering how to remove items with your admin? You can assign a Delete Record behavior in the place of Update Record. More often than not, the best way to prevent items from showing up on your Web page but not from your database is to create an "Active" column. Your Recordset Query can then check against the value in this field and knows whether or not it should be shown.

45.2

STEP 3: PREVIEW IN YOUR BROWSER

- Press **F12** on your keyboard or click the **Preview in Browser** icon on the Document Toolbar.
- Navigate to the record you want to update. Make changes in the text fields and click the **Update** button as shown in **Figure 45.3**.
- Your changes are recorded in the database. If you chose a Go To page, you will be redirected there immediately afterwards.

> **TIP**
>
> Deleting rows from a database is usually not commonly done in a Web application, because archived customer service records or sales reports may depend on that existing data. For example, if you are selling an item that is out of stock momentarily and don't want to take back orders, you shouldn't delete this sku. Saving this item as inactive lets you keep your item description and other related information until you need it again.

ONLINE RESOURCES

FIXING COMMON TESTING SERVER PROBLEMS:

Although originally written for Dreamweaver Ultradev, the majority of the solutions listed in this directory provide fixes that work with Dreamweaver MX. `www.macromedia.com/support/ultradev/troubleshoot.html`

MICROSOFT SOLUTIONS FOR HTTP 500 UPDATEABLE QUERY ERRORS:

Some documentation is available on the Macromedia site about this topic. However, this page features more in-depth information and other suggestions on how to properly tweak your sharing permissions for IUSR, such as setting permissions in your temp directory. `http://support.microsoft.com/default.aspx?scid=kb;EN-US;q175168`

45.3

CHAPTER 10

EXTEND THE FEATURES OF DREAMWEAVER WITH EXTENSIONS

Virtually all of Macromedia's new products now come bundled with an assistant application called Extension Manager. This utility enables you to install add-on functionalities to your Macromedia products. You can currently choose from 800+ Dreamweaver Extensions. Before developing a common Web site functionality, such as a shopping cart, interactive images, or an intelligent form, look for an Extension to do the work for you. There are also Extensions for common minor production tasks, such as adding filler text. Extensions can also make other programs work better with Dreamweaver. For example, you can generate Fireworks graphics within Dreamweaver with an Extension.

To browse for Dreamweaver Extensions, visit http:// exchange.macromedia.com, the Macromedia Exchange home page. Macromedia provides this site as a free service; however, you do have to register your e-mail address to become a member. Once inside, you can navigate the extensive library of Extensions by type, keyword, author, and more.

Please note that if you purchased Dreamweaver MX when it first debuted, you may have an older build of the Extension Manager. As of the publication date of this book, the latest version is v1.5.054. While not critical, you should update your Extension Manager to ensure a bug-free experience. This update is available as a free download from the Macromedia Exchange home page.

KEEPING YOUR SITE LOOKING FRESH WITH A RANDOM IMAGE GROUP

46.1 (CP 61)

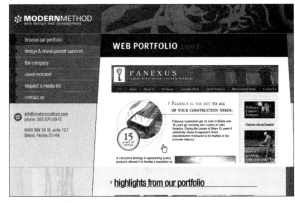

46.2 (CP 62)

NOTE

You can find the Random Images Extension on the CD-ROM.

I t's a proven fact — the best way to retain steady site traffic is to continuously update your Web site. But who's got the time to update their site many times a day? Implementing a random image Extension helps you cheat a little. As you see in **Figures 46.1 (CP 61)** and **46.2 (CP 62)**, a Web design company uses this technique to display one of ten case studies on their home page. As a result, a returning visitor can usually find a new feature on the home page even though the site hasn't changed.

STEP 1: INSTALL THE EXTENSION

The Macromedia Extension Manager must be installed prior to installing Extensions. Chances are that if Dreamweaver MX is installed, you can find Extensions under your Macromedia folder in the Windows Start menu. If Extensions is not present, it is available as a free download from www.macromedia.com for registered users. To install an extension, download or copy the MXP file to your computer and double-click it to begin the setup process.

- Browse to the Technique 46 folder on the CD-ROM.
- Double-click the file named randImage.mxp. A disclaimer dialog box appears. Read this document before proceeding.
- Click **OK** to accept the terms of the disclaimer.
- The Extension has been installed. A green checkmark appears next to its name in your Extension Manager, as shown in **Figure 46.3**.

STEP 2: RUN THE RANDOM IMAGE COMMAND

After installed, you can now run this Extension from the Dreamweaver Commands menu. As with any technique involving graphics, you need to prepare your graphics and save your document before starting this technique so that image paths can be properly linked.

NOTE

Some vendors may reuse common elements in their Extensions, which may prompt you to override files while installing. For example, if you install any other Extensions from Kaosweaver, maker of this Advanced Random Image Extension, the installer will ask you if you want to override a .gif file. You can always click **OK** to proceed — it's the same file.

- Create a new Web page in Dreamweaver MX. Save your document.
- Choose **View ➢ Visual Aids ➢ Invisible Elements** to enable Visual Aids. If Visual Aids is already checked, proceed to the next step.
- Choose **Commands ➢ Kaosweaver.com ➢ Advanced Random Images**. A dialog box appears (see **Figure 46.4**).

NOTE

If Advanced Random Images is grayed out (i.e., not available) make sure of two things. First, check that the extension was installed and is active. To do this, use the Extension Manager. There should be a checkmark, as shown in Figure 46.3. Second, you may not have saved your page. Save the page now using **File ➢ Save As**.

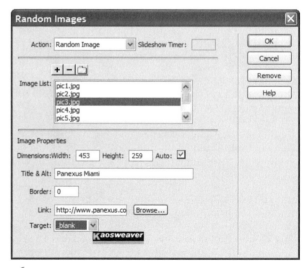

46.4

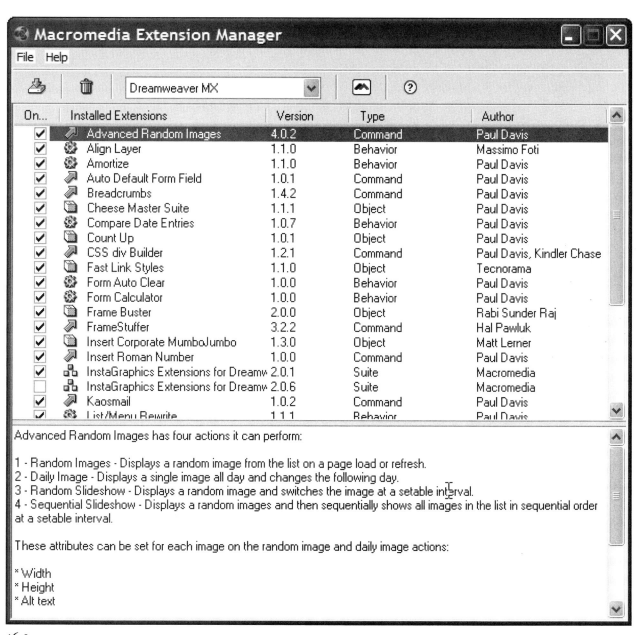

46.3

- Choose an action. For this example, choose **Random Images**. The four options produce similar results.

  - **Random Images:** Displays a random image when a page is loaded or refreshed. You must specify a pool of images from which it cycles.
  - **Daily Image:** Displays a single image all day. The image is changed every 24 hours sequentially from a specified selection of images.
  - **Random Slideshow:** Displays a random image and switches the image randomly at an adjustable interval, set in seconds.
  - **Sequential Slideshow:** Starts by displaying a random image from your specified image selection and then cycles images sequentially.

- Click the **Plus Sign** (+) button to add an image to your list. If you change your mind, you can remove images from your list with the **Minus Sign** (–) button. To add all images contained in a specified folder, use the **Browse** button. At least two images must be selected to view results in Step 3.

- Set image dimensions for each image manually or check the Auto box to have

Dreamweaver automatically fill these values in for you.

- Optionally, you can set individual specifications for Title & Alt, Border, Link, and Target. When making these entries, do not insert special characters, such as apostrophes: They may disrupt the JavaScript code generated by the Extension.

- Click **OK** to complete the command. A warning appears, asking you to enable visual aids to see the inserted object. Click **OK** to continue because you already did this earlier in this step.

- A yellow invisible element icon appears on your screen. You may position it where you want the random image to appear.

STEP 3: PREVIEW IN YOUR BROWSER

- Press **F12** on your keyboard or click the **Preview in Browser** icon on the Document Toolbar.
- Click the **Refresh** button to view a random image each time the page is loaded.

NOTE

The fields available in the dialog box for this Extension change based on the Action you choose. For example, if you choose Random Slideshow or Sequential Slide Show, you won't be able to specify a URL or image properties for each image, but the Slideshow Timer field will be enabled.

NOTE

This Extension inserts an `OnLoad` event in the body tag if you choose either of the two slideshow actions. If you change your mind about the action on the page and want to convert it to a random image, you may need to manually remove that code to prevent an error message. If you have not saved your document, Undo should do the trick.

ACCEPTING CREDIT CARD PAYMENTS WITH PAYPAL SHOPPING CART

47.1 (CP 63)

47.2 (CP 64)

PayPal is a popular service that allows people to send and receive money online. Its most popular feature is the ability to let average people accept credit card payments online for a small per-transaction fee and without a merchant account. PayPal offers an off-site hosted shopping cart service, meaning that you don't need to worry about installing any server software or CGI scripts. Your site doesn't even need to be secure because financial transactions occur on PayPal's servers. You simply plug their shopping cart HTML code and use the buy buttons that appear on your page, as shown in **Figures 47.1 (CP 63)** and **47.2 (CP 64)**.

To complete this technique, you must have a PayPal ID. To become a PayPal member, visit `www.PayPal.com` and complete the sign-up process. After becoming a PayPal member, you need to link a bank account to your PayPal account in order to receive credit card deposits. PayPal offers other financial arrangements as well — for more information, visit their Web site. To install an extension, download or copy the MXP file to your computer and double-click it to begin the setup process.

STEP 1: INSTALL THE EXTENSION

To install an extension, download or copy the MXP file to your computer and double-click it to begin the setup process.

- Browse to the Technique 47 folder on the CD-ROM.
- Double-click the file named KW_PayPalButtons.mxp. A disclaimer dialog box appears. Read this document before proceeding.
- Click **OK** to accept the terms of the disclaimer.
- The Extension has been installed. A green checkmark is next to its name in your Extension Manager.

STEP 2: CONFIGURE THE PAYPAL CART MAIN MENU

This Extension's dialog box has more than one screen, because there are a lot of possible configuration options. This step covers the Main menu, which gives you the option of branding PayPal's cart with your company information.

- Create a new Web page.
- Choose **Commands** ➢ **PayPal Shopping Cart.** A dialog box appears, showing the Main submenu screen (see **Figure 47.3**).

> **REMINDER**
>
> The Macromedia Extension Manager must be installed in order for this Extension to work. If you do not have Extension Manager installed, you can find it on the Dreamweaver CD-ROM, or you can download it for free on the Macromedia Exchange Web site.

- Enter your Site domain name. You should include the `http://` protocol in the URL to make it an absolute URL. Example:

`http://www.YourSiteHere.com`

- Enter your PayPal ID. This is the e-mail address you registered as your member name with PayPal. If you don't have a PayPal account yet, click the **Get PayPal** button and follow the sign-up process.
- Optionally, enter your Logo URL. This URL should point to a 150 x 50 picture file on your server, typically a JPG or GIF. The URL must be absolute, as shown in Figure 47.3. Example:

`http://www.YourSiteHere.com/images/`
`logo.gif`

- Optionally, enter the Cancel URL. This is a Web page on your server where PayPal can redirect a customer that has forfeited an order in the middle

> **WARNING**
>
> Do not click **OK** before completing the next two steps. This is a multipage dialog box, so other values have to be entered before you execute the command. Otherwise, an incomplete configuration will result, and you'll have to start over.

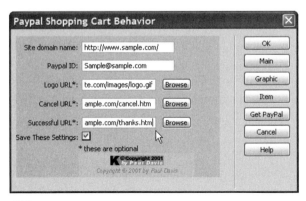

47.3

of the checkout process. Your Cancel URL page can inform customers of alternative ordering methods or feature bargains to lure them back to shopping. Just as the previous URLs, it must be absolute:

```
http://www.YourSiteHere.com/
cancel.html
```

■ Optionally, enter the Successful URL. Many sites create a "thank you for shopping" page for this field. Others use this opportunity to collect customer feedback about the shopping process by creating a page with a form. Whatever you decide, make it an absolute URL:

```
http://www.YourSiteHere.com/
thanks.html
```

STEP 3: CHOOSE YOUR BUY BUTTON

The buy button is the most important component of the online store. When clicked, it tells the cart to add a particular item to your shopping cart. PayPal includes various designs (shown in **Figure 47.4**) that you can use, or you can create your own for a personalized look.

■ Click the **Graphic** button. The Graphic submenu screen appears, as shown in Figure 47.4.

■ Choose a button graphic style by selecting a radio button.

■ If you want to use a custom buy button graphic, choose the first option, browse to your graphic, and select it.

STEP 4: ENTER THE DETAILS OF AN ITEM FOR SALE

The Item Details menu allows you to set the parameters for the sale. This Extension only inserts a programmed buy button (link) on your page. You need to enter the details of the item on your Web page once again so that people can see it.

■ Click the **Item** button. The Item submenu screen appears, as shown in **Figure 47.5**.

> **TIP**
>
> The buy button graphic can be any size. For best results, use a GIF with a transparent background around the shape. Also, this URL can be relative or absolute. Unlike the entries in the Main menu, the location of your buy button is not passed to the PayPal server for display on their pages.

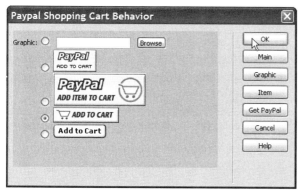

47.4

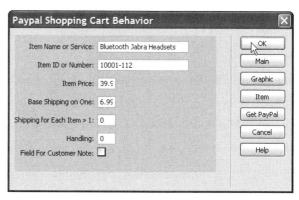

47.5

- Enter the Item Name or Service. This name is displayed in the cart.
- Enter the Item ID or Number. This can be your SKU number, which also appears in the cart.
- Enter the individual Item Price. (Note: People can modify quantities within the shopping cart pop-up later.)
- Enter a numerical value for Base Shipping on One. This is your flat shipping rate for a single quantity of this item. If you offer free shipping, enter **0**.
- Enter a value for Each Item Greater than One. You can offer a discounted rate for multiple item buys or enter the same value as your Base Shipping cost. This step is optional.
- Enter a Handling fee. If you offer free handling, enter **0**.
- Click **OK** to insert the PayPal shopping cart buy button.

TIP

If your inventory specs are already in a database, you should modify the outputted code to receive dynamic variables. Remember, this PayPal cart Extension is essentially a URL builder — it sends all of your items specs to the PayPal server as a QueryString. All you have to do is view the source of the page, find the button link, and replace the static values in your RecordSet entries. (Don't forget to duplicate these Recordset entries in your design area as well.) After you master this, try adding this functionality to the Master/Detail template set explained in Chapter 9. With a little work, you'll have a truly automated shopping cart system built in no time!

STEP 5: PREVIEW IN YOUR BROWSER

- Press **F12** on your keyboard or click the **Preview in Browser** icon on the Document Toolbar.
- Click your buy button to add the item to your shopping cart. A PayPal cart appears in a pop-up window, as shown in **Figure 47.6**.
- Follow the steps in the pop-up cart window to complete the purchase.

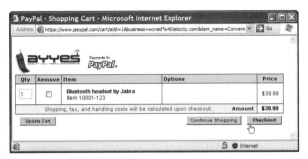

47.6

NOTE

To add more items to your site, choose **Commands ➤ PayPal Shopping Cart** again and skip to Step 4. The Extension remembers your settings on the Main and Graphic submenu screens from your previous selections.

WARNING

The sample included on the CD-ROM contains a fictional PayPal ID and is a fictional store, so as a result the buy button won't allow you to open the example. To view a great example of a real PayPal store, visit `www.petals fragrances.com`.

DON'T GET FRAMED! USE FRAME BUSTER TO BREAK FREE

48.1

48.2

Is your Web site a victim of third-party framing? Some sites on the Web have been known to frame other Web site's content as the body of their pages. **Figure 48.1** shows how a portal has linked directly into an external site from its frameset. In most cases, this may confuse site visitors, who may think that the framed page belongs to the framing site. You can prevent and protect your site from this activity with the Frame Buster Extension, as shown in **Figure 48.2**. This object inserts defensive JavaScript code that detects frames and closes them immediately, leaving only your protected page on-screen.

STEP 1: INSTALL THE EXTENSION

Using technology to stop framing sites is easy and more cost effective than taking legal action. After the object is installed, it requires no maintenance and stops offenders in their tracks, whether you're aware of them or not. To install an Extension, download or copy the MXP file to your computer and double-click it to begin the setup process.

■ Go to www.dreamweaver-extension.com.
■ Download the Frame Buster Extension. A disclaimer dialog box appears. Read this document before proceeding.
■ Click **OK** to accept the terms of the disclaimer.

■ The Extension has been installed. A green checkmark appears next to its name in your Extension Manager.

STEP 2: INSERT THE FRAME BUSTER OBJECT

Frame Buster is different from the Extensions in the preceding techniques because it is an object. There is nothing to configure — Frame Buster simply inserts a chunk of ready-made JavaScript code before your HEAD tags, as shown in **Figure 48.3**.

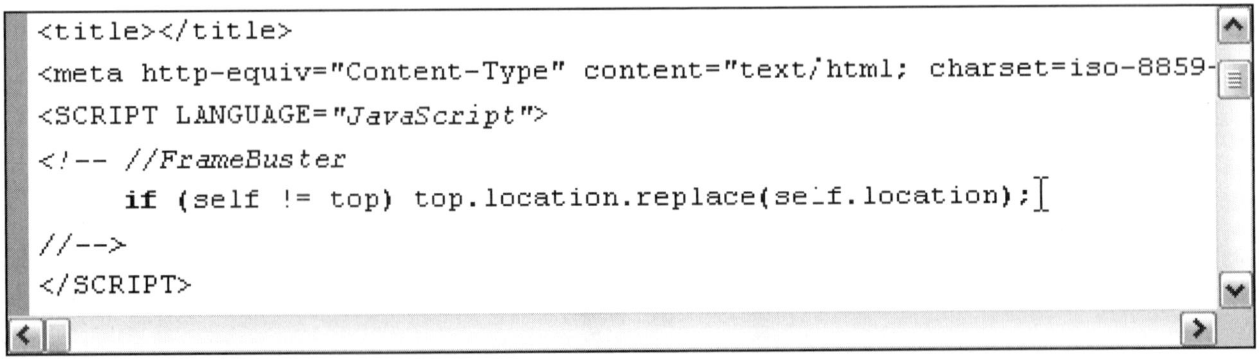

```
<title></title>
<meta http-equiv="Content-Type" content="text/html; charset=iso-8859-
<SCRIPT LANGUAGE="JavaScript">
<!-- //FrameBuster
    if (self != top) top.location.replace(self.location);
//-->
</SCRIPT>
```

48.3

Don't Get Framed! Use Frame Buster to Break Free

229

- Open the Web page that you want to protect with Frame Buster.
- Choose **Insert ➤ Frame Buster**. It appears at the bottom of the Objects menu, along with any other Objects you installed.
- A dialog box appears. To insert the object, click **OK**, as shown in **Figure 48.4**.

NOTE

The code for this object resides above the BODY tag, so as a result the Frame Buster code is invisible in the Design View mode of Dreamweaver. To remove this object, switch to Code View and scroll to the top of your document. You find some comment tags surrounding the Frame Buster code with its name. Delete everything in between, including the SCRIPT tags. Also note that if the words "Frame Buster" appear anywhere in the document, the extension won't insert the code because it will assume it already exists.

TIP

Frame Buster is intended for a non-frames site to defend itself from a framing site. If you built your site using frames and are having problems with other sites framing yours, you should migrate to a dynamic "include file" architecture to get rid of your frames. Include files enable your application server to import code from external documents into one, similar to how frames are managed. For more information about include files, search for Server-Side Includes in the Dreamweaver help system (press **F1**).

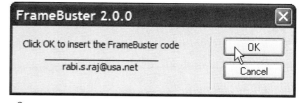

48.4

STEP 3: TEST THE FRAME BUSTER

- Save your Frame Buster protected Web page and close it.
- Open a frameset. You can find a sample frameset on the CD-ROM.
- Change a link on the Frameset menu to point to your protected Web page. Set the Target to open within the frame body of the frameset.

- Choose **File ➤ Save All** to save all Web pages.
- Press **F12** on your keyboard or click the **Preview in Browser** icon on the Document Toolbar.
- Click the link that opens your Web page in the frameset.
- Frame Buster quickly breaks your page out of the frameset, as shown in **Figure 48.5**.

48.5

PREVENTING ORPHANED FRAME CONTENT WITH FRAMESTUFFER

49.1 (CP 65)

49.2 (CP 66)

NOTE

You can find the FrameStuffer Extension and the example used in this technique in the folder named Technique 49 on the CD-ROM.

Frames enable you to show multiple Web pages simultaneously on the screen. However, HTML does not form dependant relationships for the pages that make up a frameset. As a result, linking to a frame may result in an orphaned page. Usually, a content page appears without its menu, as shown in **Figure 49.1** (**CP 65**). Orphaned pages occur most frequently when a page is accessed from external links from search engines. To prevent this, you can use the FrameStuffer Extension. Orphaned pages then are able to detect the absence of their parent frame and stuff themselves inside as intended, as shown in **Figure 49.2** (**CP 66**).

STEP 1: INSTALL THE EXTENSION

To install an Extension, download or copy the MXP file to your computer and double click it to begin the setup process.

- Browse to the Technique 49 folder on the CD-ROM.
- Double-click the file named FrameJammer. mxp. A disclaimer dialog box appears. Read this document before proceeding.
- Click **OK** to accept the terms of the disclaimer.
- The Extension has been installed. A green checkmark appears next to its name in your Extension Manager.

STEP 2: PREPARE THE FRAMESET

FrameStuffer records the default body value (page) on the Frameset page and adds JavaScript that responds to orphan "stuff requests."

- Create a frameset or open an existing frameset.
- Name each frame if you have not already done so.
- Click the body page or any page you want to prevent from being orphaned.
- Save your Web page. FrameStuffer won't run unless the page is saved.
- Choose **Command** ➢ **Dabbler** ➢ **FrameStuffer**. A dialog box appears, as shown in **Figure 49.3**.

- Click **Browse** to choose the frameset (usually the one that's currently open). The names of the frames in this frameset appear in the lower drop-down menu.

WARNING

FrameStuffer's built-in code uses a variable name called "booker_". Do not use this name for your frames because it may make FrameStuffer fail or produce errors. More information about this is available in the FrameStuffer documentation, which can be accessed by clicking Help from the FrameStuffer dialog box.

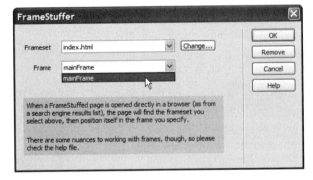

49.3

- Choose the target frame, as shown in Figure 49.3.
- Click **OK**.
- Save and close the frameset.

STEP 3: PREVIEW IN YOUR BROWSER

- Close all of your documents, open the body frame, and then press **F12**.
- FrameStuffer instantly surrounds the body frame with its dependant frameset, as shown in **Figure 49.4**.

TIP

FrameStuffer is written in JavaScript, so its source is totally open to customization. For example, its documentation explains how to use FrameStuffer to jump to an anchor by modifying its code. It also suggests code changes to ensure better compatibility with Dreamweaver templates. For more information, refer to FrameStuffer Help.

49.4

GENERATING IMAGES WITHIN DREAMWEAVER WITH INSTAGRAPHICS

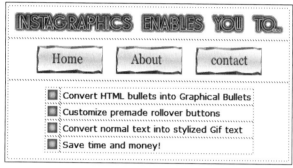

50.1

NOTE

You can find the example used in this technique in the folder named Technique 50 on the CD-ROM. Note: Extension Manager prevents you from installing this Extension unless Fireworks 4 or greater is installed on your system first.

InstaGraphics is a suite of objects and commands rolled up into one powerful Extension. After installed, it adds three dynamic image-generating features previously native to Fireworks. You can insert customizable premade rollover buttons, convert text on your Web page into GIF text graphics, and convert default HTML bullets into attractive image bullets. All of the graphics in **Figure 50.1** were generated within Dreamweaver by converting existing text elements. The following steps show you how to create this page.

STEP 1: INSTALL THE EXTENSION

To install an Extension, download or copy the MXP file to your computer and double-click it to begin the setup process. Remember, you'll need either Fireworks 4 or Fireworks MX to use this Extension.

- Go to www.macromedia.com/software/ dreamweaver/productinfo/extend/ insta.html.
- Download the InstaGraphics Extension. A disclaimer dialog box appears. Read this document before proceeding.
- Click **OK** to accept the terms of the disclaimer.
- The Extension has been installed. A green checkmark appears next to its name in your Extension Manager.

STEP 2: GENERATE TEXT GRAPHICS

The Convert Text to Images feature in InstaGraphics lets you create GIF text directly from Dreamweaver. You can now freely use nonstandard Web fonts and dress them with the 30 premade text styles included. It also has the ability to mass-replace text within

specified tags into images, such as the heading shown in Figure 50.1.

- Save your Web page.
- Type some text on your page using **Heading 1**, found in the Property inspector.
- Choose **Commands ➢ Convert Text to Images**. A dialog box appears (see **Figure 50.2**).
- Choose **H1** from the Convert menu because the text you created was formatted as Heading 1. If you want to manipulate other tags or a highlighted selection instead, you may do so by selecting the other radio buttons.
- Choose a Fireworks Style from the pull-down menu. A preview of the style appears when you change the selection.
- Choose a Font. Please note that the preview image won't change with your font selection and

---

TIP

InstaGraphics commands and objects run at optimal speed when Fireworks is open and running in the background. Simply start the application and switch back to Dreamweaver before moving on to the next step. Otherwise, it will attempt to launch Fireworks every time you run one of its three functions.

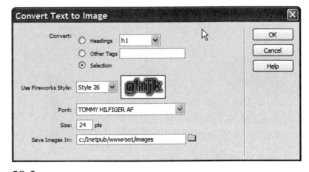

50.2

that you cannot select certain types of Type 1 PostScript fonts.

■ Enter the desired point size of your font in the Size menu.

■ If you want to save your images in a directory other than where the Web page was saved, use the **Browse** button. Navigate to the folder of your choice and press the **Select** button to close the Pick Folder dialog box.

■ Click **OK** to generate the graphics.

STEP 3: CONVERT HTML BULLETS INTO GRAPHICS

Bored of the bullet HTML circle character? You can breathe new life into your unordered bulleted lists with the Convert Bullet to Images command. This feature generates a bullet design based on your specs, deletes your old bullets, inserts an invisible two column table, and inserts your text into individual rows to the right of the images.

■ Create a bulleted list of text by using the **Unordered List** button in the Property inspector.

■ Choose **Commands** ➢ **Convert Text to Images**. A dialog box appears (see **Figure 50.3**).

■ Choose **Unordered List** from the Convert menu. This converts all unordered lists on your page. Alternatively, you can choose Current List to just change the bulleted list your cursor was on prior to running this command.

■ Optionally, you can uncheck the Table to Align Bullets and Text option. This choice is good

WARNING

InstaGraphics is extremely picky about special characters in folder paths. Be sure not to include any kind of special ASCII character in your site folder or save the image path, or Dreamweaver will report that it cannot find the file and fail mid-process. Also note that deleting the graphics in Dreamweaver or using Undo won't delete the PNG and GIF graphics from your hard drive.

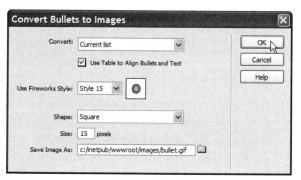

50.3

if you intend to create small bullets, as shown in Figure 50.3.

■ Choose a Fireworks Style from the pull-down menu. A preview of the graphic appears on the right-hand side of the menu.

■ Choose a bullet shape from the Shape menu. This selection won't change the image preview — you only see the results when the command is executed.

■ Choose the Size of the bullet in pixels. A good bullet size is 6 to 12 pixels.

■ Enter an image name in the Save Image As field. If you want to override an existing bullet image, click the **Browse** button and navigate to the file.

■ Click **OK** to generate your image bullets.

STEP 4: CREATE ROLLOVER FIREWORKS BUTTONS

InstaGraphics adds another instant button solution to Dreamweaver with its own Fireworks button

TIP

These graphical bullets do not possess the auto-indent, auto-wrap properties of HTML bullets. This is because they are essentially just images combined with table formatting rules or align-ment rules (middle) if you don't select the table option. Expect to make some modifications to their presentation if your text wraps, such as using hard enters to control the text or adding vertical padding to position the bullet within the cell correctly.

menu. Similar to the Flash menu technique in Chapter 3, this object allows you choose from a list of premade button styles and customize them with your text by using dialog boxes, as shown in **Figure 50.4**.

■ Choose **Insert ➢ Interactive Images ➢ Fireworks Button**. A dialog box appears (see Figure 50.4).

■ Choose a button Style. A preview appears in the Sample window.

■ Enter a Button Width in pixels.

■ Enter a Text Label. This is the text that appears inside your button.

■ Choose a Font. If you don't select a font, the designer's default font, which is pictured in the Sample preview, will be selected for you.

NOTE

Some of the intended fonts for the premade Fireworks buttons may not be installed in your system, so as a result the designs may not look like the designer originally intended. In my case, the dialog box warned me that I did not have the Berkeley font for the Scroll style or the Sand font for the Surfboard style. These fonts are available at various type foundries on the Web; however, they are not required. If you do not make another selection in the Font menu, Fireworks will prompt you to choose a substi-tute font in the image generation process. If you click the **No Change** button, Arial will be selected for you.

- Choose a font Size. A recommended value is filled in for you based on the selected Style.
- Enter this button's Link or click the **Browse** button to select a page from your site. Choose a target from the drop-down menu if appropriate.
- Select a folder to save your images to by pressing the **Browse** button and navigating to the desired folder.
- Name your button in the Base File Name field. Two images are created with this name in the specified folder — one for mouse up and one for mouse out states.
- Click **OK** to generate your Fireworks buttons.

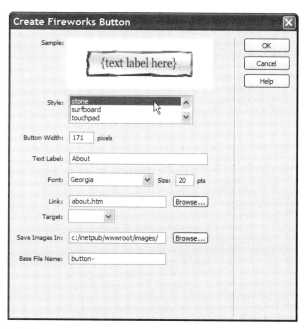

50.4

APPENDIX A
WHAT'S ON THE CD-ROM

This appendix provides you with information on the contents of the CD that accompanies this book. For the latest and greatest information, please refer to the ReadMe file located at the root of the CD. Here is what you will find:

- System Requirements
- CD-ROM Installation Instructions
- What's on the CD-ROM
- Troubleshooting

SYSTEM REQUIREMENTS

Make sure that your computer meets the minimum system requirements listed in this section. If your computer doesn't match up to most of these requirements, you may have a problem using the contents of the CD.

FOR WINDOWS 9X, WINDOWS 2000, WINDOWS NT4 (WITH SP 4 OR LATER), WINDOWS ME, OR WINDOWS XP:

- PC with a Pentium processor running at 120 MHz or faster
- At least 32MB of total RAM installed on your computer; for best performance, we recommend at least 64MB
- Ethernet network interface card (NIC) or modem with a speed of at least 28,800 bps
- A CD-ROM drive

FOR MACINTOSH:

- Mac OS computer with a 68040 or faster processor running OS 7.6 or later
- At least 32MB of total RAM installed on your computer; for best performance, we recommend at least 64MB
- Ethernet network interface card (NIC) or modem with a speed of at least 28,800 bps
- A CD-ROM drive

CD-ROM INSTALLATION INSTRUCTIONS

To install a particular piece of software, open its folder with My Computer or Internet Explorer. What you do next depends on what you find in the software's folder:

1. First, look for a ReadMe.txt file or a .doc or .htm document. If this is present, it should contain installation instructions and other useful information.

2. If the folder contains an executable (.exe) file, this is usually an installation program. Often it will be called Setup.exe or Install.exe, but in some cases the filename reflects an abbreviated version of the software's name and version number. Run the .exe file to start the installation process.

WHAT'S ON THE CD-ROM

The following sections provide a summary of the software and other materials you'll find on the CD.

50 TECHNIQUES

The 50 Fast Dreamweaver MX Techniques CD-ROM contains working Web pages for each technique showcased in the book. A variety of files, including Fireworks graphics, Flash movies, database files, and graphics can be found on the disc.

APPLICATIONS

The following applications are on the CD:

Shareware programs are fully functional, trial versions of copyrighted programs. If you like particular programs, register with their authors for a nominal fee and receive licenses, enhanced versions, and technical support. *Freeware programs* are copyrighted games, applications, and utilities that are free for personal use. Unlike shareware, these programs do not require a fee or provide technical support. *GNU software* is governed by its own license, which is included inside the folder of the GNU product. See the GNU license for more details.

Trial, demo, or evaluation versions are usually limited either by time or functionality (such as being unable to save projects). Some trial versions are very sensitive to system date changes. If you alter your computer's date, the programs will "time out" and will no longer be functional.

You can connect directly to these Web sites by clicking the appropriate hyperlink in the HTML interface on the CD-ROM that accompanies this book.

Dreamweaver MX from Macromedia

30-day trial version for Windows and Macintosh. Dreamweaver MX is an easy to use, full-featured, visual Web development program. For more information, check out `www.macromedia.com/software/dreamweaver`.

Flash MX from Macromedia

30-day trial version for Windows and Macintosh. Flash has become the animation standard for the Web. This latest installment features vast improvements for building dynamic content with a brand new interface. For more information, visit `www.macromedia.com/software/flash`.

Fireworks MX from Macromedia

30-day trial version for Windows and Macintosh. Fireworks is a graphic design application specifically designed for designing Web sites and making image editing within Dreamweaver possible. For more information, check out `www.macromedia.com/software/fireworks`.

Acrobat Reader from Adobe

Free version for Windows and Macintosh. Acrobat Reader allows you to view PDF files and eBook files from your computer. For more information visit `www.adobe.com/products/acrobat`.

Framestuffer from Hal Pawluk

Freeware version for Windows. Framed pages opened "naked" outside their frameset find the frameset and position themselves in the correct frame.

HTML Rename! from Expandable Language

Shareware version for Windows and Macintosh. This cross-platform utility augments your HTML editor by generating universally compatible filenames and fixing URL links. Using HTML Rename before you transfer files saves you from the need to repair mangled filenames, broken links, and extra or missing carriage returns in text files.

PayPal Cart from Paul Davis

This free extension adds the needed script for PayPal Shopping Cart and retains your default information for quicker reentry.

Random Images from Paul Davis

Display random images, daily images, or slideshows with this handy extension.

EBOOK VERSION OF *50 FAST DREAMWEAVER MX TECHNIQUES*

The complete text of this book is on the CD in Adobe's Portable Document Format (PDF). You can read and search through the file with the Adobe Acrobat Reader (also included on the CD).

TROUBLESHOOTING

If you have difficulty installing or using any of the materials on the companion CD, try the following solutions:

- **Turn off any anti-virus software that you may have running.** Installers sometimes mimic virus activity and can make your computer incorrectly believe that it is being infected by a virus. (Be sure to turn the anti-virus software back on later.)
- **Close all running programs.** The more programs you're running, the less memory is available to other programs. Installers also typically update files and programs; if you keep other programs running, installation may not work properly.
- **Reference the ReadMe:** Please refer to the ReadMe file located at the root of the CD-ROM for the latest product information at the time of publication.

If you still have trouble with the CD, please call the Customer Care phone number: (800) 762-2974. Outside the United States, call 1 (317) 572-3994. You can also contact Wiley Customer Care by e-mail at `techsupdum@wiley.com`. Wiley will provide technical support only for installation and other general quality control items; for technical support on the applications themselves, consult the program's vendor or author.

APPENDIX B
LEARNING MORE ON THE WEB

Just when you figure out all of the coolest, latest developments on the Web, something new comes along. Fortunately, one of the best ways to keep up with Web design is to look for information on the Internet itself.

I try to visit a few Web sites regularly to keep up with emerging technologies, research on interface design, and the latest developments, such as Dynamic HTML, XML, and the many other aspects of Web development. The following sites are in alphabetical order (because that's supposed to be fair). I recommend you take a quick look at all of them and then bookmark the ones you like best so that you can return to them easily.

You can connect directly to these Web sites by clicking the appropriate hyperlink in the HTML interface on the CD-ROM that accompanies this book.

ADOBE SYSTEMS, INC.

`www.adobe.com`
Adobe is not only a great resource for graphics and other products, but its Web site features an impressive collection of design tips and strategies for creating graphics for the Web, in addition to well-designed HTML pages.

ART AND THE ZEN OF WEB SITES

`www.tlc-systems.com/webtips.shtml`
As the name implies, this site shows you the way to simple yet powerful Web design, and it has a great collection of quotes (but I have to wonder, did those people really say those things?).

CNET

`www.cnet.com`
CNET gives you news about all aspects of the Web, as well as in-depth reports on new technologies and other news affecting Web designers. CNET also has extensive software libraries for both Windows and Macintosh platforms.

COMMUNICATION ARTS INTERACTIVE

`www.commarts.com`
Looking for creative ideas? Need some design guidance or a few tips on how to develop the best graphics for your site? Point your browser in the direction of Communication Arts Interactive.

THE DIRECTORY

`www.thedirectory.org`

Looking for an Internet service provider? Look no further. The Directory is a comprehensive guide to ISPs on the Net, featuring a searchable database with thousands of ISPs worldwide.

DMX ZONE

`www.dmxzone.net`

This is a great Web site maintained by and for the Dreamweaver MX User Community. You find tutorials, Extensions, and answers to lots of your questions here. You can also contribute content to the site to share with other Dreamweaver MX users.

DREAMWEAVER EXTENSIONS DATABASE

`www.idest.com/cgi-bin/database.cgi`

This site has a vast searchable database of Dreamweaver Extensions, including objects, behaviors, templates, commands, and techniques for extending Dreamweaver — all downloadable from the Web. (Note: If you're still not sure what Dreamweaver Extensions are, you can skip this site for now — it's for advanced Dreamweaver users.)

FLASHKIT

`www.flashkit.com`

Visit Flashkit to find news, tutorials, source files, shareware, and tips about Flash MX and Action Script. Contributions to the site by other Flash MX users are also encouraged here!

THE HTML WRITERS GUILD

`www.hwg.org`

This Web site is an international organization of World Wide Web designers and Internet publishing professionals. The site includes a variety of HTML resources, as well as Web business mailing lists, information repositories, and a chance to interact with peers.

INTERNET.COM

`www.internet.com`

This site has so many great resources it's hard to know where to start. On the main page, you find comprehensive news coverage of events, legal issues, and trends that are shaping the way we work, live, and use technology.

Visit the Web Developers section to find a wealth of information about Web design, including technical issues, design, and information about software, from development tools to Web browsers.

THE MACROMEDIA DESIGNERS AND DEVELOPERS CENTER

`www.macromedia.com`
The Macromedia Web site is worth a regular visit. Not only do you find product updates and other helpful information about Macromedia software, you also find many great resources for designers.

The Macromedia official help center is filled with tutorials, samples, and other assets designed to keep developers up-to-date, especially if you use its programs, such as Dreamweaver, Fireworks, Freehand, and Flash.

NETSCAPE

`www.netscape.com`
Keep your eye on the Netscape site for updates to Navigator, as well as the latest on how it will support new features on the Web.

PROJECT COOL AND DEVX

`www.projectcool.com` or `www.devx.com`
One of my all-time favorite Web sites, Project Cool is dedicated to helping anyone become a better Web designer. Now that Project Cool and DevX are one, you can find a ton of great resources all in one place.

The creators of the Project Cool site have always had a talent for sharing great Web design tips and showcasing the best of the Web. The site also does a great job of keeping up with the latest developments, such as DHTML and Cascading Style Sheets.

SEARCH ENGINE HELP

`www.searchenginehelp.com`
If you're confused about how to submit your site to search engines, or you want to get better placement in the search engines where your site already appears, Search Engine Help can give you all the tips and ideas you have time to study and implement. These are the pros with the most updated tips on how to get your site the best placement possible in all the most important search engines.

TECHNET

`www.technet.com`
Watch the Microsoft developer's site for updates to Internet Explorer, as well as information on how it will support new features on the Web.

WEBMONKEY

`www.webmonkey.com`
Tune up your browser and make sure your Web site is up to snuff at the HotWired WebMonkey site. You can use its online diagnostic tools to test your browser and find out about plug-ins and other Web development tools. You can also find HTML tutorials and other Web design references.

WILEY PUBLISHING

`www.wiley.com`
Wiley Publishing offers a wide range of books on Web design (including this one!) and features links to great magazines and other resources for Web designers.

THE WORLD WIDE WEB ARTISTS CONSORTIUM

`www.wwwac.org`
Better known as the WWWAC, this nonprofit, member-supported organization of Web designers keeps you up-to-date on current Web design issues when you subscribe to its e-mail list. But, as with any mailing list, make sure that you read a few weeks' worth of messages before you post one of your own. More than 1,000 people share their ideas on the WWWAC list, including some of the most respected designers on the Web.

WORLD WIDE WEB CONSORTIUM

`www.w3.org`
The official source for HTML updates, the W3C sets the standards for HTML code. At this site, you find all of the published HTML specifications, as well as a wide range of resources for Web developers.

ZDNET

`www.zdnet.com` or `www.cnet.com`
Another great technology news site. ZDNet is now owned by CNET, but the two sites feature different resources and references and are both worth the visit. ZDNet is the more technical of the two, designed more for developers, while CNET has more of a consumer focus.

EXTENDING THE FEATURES OF DREAMWEAVER MX

Instead of waiting around for the next version of Dreamweaver to catch up with the bleeding edge technologies and techniques emerging every day, you can add new features to the program this very minute with Dreamweaver Extensions—most of which are absolutely free to use. Simply log on to `http://exchange.macromedia.com`, fill out the member registration form, and visit the Dreamweaver MX section to browse their 600+ and growing Extension inventory.

You can connect directly to these Web sites by clicking the appropriate hyperlink in the HTML interface on the CD-ROM that accompanies this book.

The following list represents Extensions I've found especially useful in recent projects:

FRAME BUSTER

Some Web sites keep one of their frames open, while they display your pages. Your visitors may think that your pages actually belong or are associated with the site that framed you. This Extension inserts the required JavaScript code to close all frames, except the one running the script through the use of a redirect.

Developer: Rabi Sunder Raj

URL: `www.geocities.com/siliconvalley/garage/2001/dreamweaver`

FRAMESTUFFER

Direct links, often by search engines, can cause your framed pages to be opened or "naked" outside their frameset. This can spell trouble if your site navigation or supporting pages are in a missing frame. The FrameStuffer Extension can find the frameset and position the parent document in its correct frame.

Developer: Hal Pawluk

URL: `www.pawluk.com/public`

INSTAGRAPHICS

Create Fireworks Web graphics, directly from Macromedia Dreamweaver — without expert design skills.

Developer: Dreamweaver

URL: `www.macromedia.com/software/dreamweaver/productinfo/extend/insta.html`

MUMBO JUMBO

This Extension inserts placeholder text into your Web pages by generating corporate technology geek-speak, which is quite humorous and useful when your clients don't provide copy.

 Developer: Macromedia

 URL: (member protected). Log on and browse the Text category of `http://exchange.macromedia.com`

PAYPAL SHOPPING CART

Inserts the PayPal shopping cart tags in the page and saves the common entered data. Unlike other PayPal Extensions available, this one has no limits and no charges.

 Developer: Paul Davis of Kaosweaver

 URL: `www.kaosweaver.com`

RANDOM IMAGES

Random Images allows you to display random images on your Web page every time the document is loaded. This highly configurable Extension can also be set to display daily images or slideshows.

 Developer: Paul Davis of Kaosweaver

 URL: `www.kaosweaver.com`

FIXING COMMON TESTING SERVER PROBLEMS:

Although originally written for Dreamweaver Ultradev, the majority of the solutions listed in this directory provide fixes that work with Dreamweaver MX.

 URL: `www.macromedia.com/support/ultradev/troubleshoot.html`

MICROSOFT SOLUTIONS FOR HTTP 500 UPDATABLE QUERY ERRORS:

Some documentation is available on the Macromedia site about this topic; however, this page features more in-depth information and other suggestions on how to properly tweak your sharing permissions for IUSR (such as setting permissions in your temp directory).

 URL: `http://support.microsoft.com/default.aspx?scid=kb;EN-US;q175168`

ABOUT THE AUTHORS

Janine Warner is an author, newspaper columnist, and university instructor.

Her many books about the Internet include *Dreamweaver MX For Dummies, Contribute For Dummies*, and *Managing Web Projects For Dummies*. She also teaches a Dreamweaver course at the University of Southern California in the Annenberg School for Communications.

A frequent speaker at industry events in the U.S. and abroad, Janine's syndicated newspaper column, "Beyond The Net," appears in print and online, including in the *Miami Herald*.

Janine draws on many years of Internet experience and has managed a wide range of Web projects. From 1994 to 1998, she ran Visiontec Communications, a Web design company that served such diverse clients as Levi Strauss & Company, Airtouch International, and ConnectMedia.

From 1998 to 2000, she worked for the *Miami Herald,* first as their Online Managing Editor, and later as Director of New Media, managing a team of designers, programmers, journalists, and sales and marketing staff. She also served as Director of Latin American Operations for CNET Networks, an international technology media company.

An award-winning former reporter, Janine earned a degree in journalism and Spanish from the University of Massachusetts, Amherst, and worked for several years in northern California as a reporter and editor. She speaks fluent Spanish and some Portuguese. To learn more, visit www.janinewarner.com.

Ivonne Berkowitz is the coauthor of *Dreamweaver MX For Dummies* and is a Web and graphic designer for PBS&J, one of the nation's top-ranked engineering firms.

She also consults for ModernMethod, a Web design firm that has worked on projects for numerous clients, including the Orange Bowl Committee, TeRespondo, and Big Wheel Cycle.

Ivonne's strengths include graphic design for the Web, Web site planning, Flash animation, and logo design. Ivonne's Web design talents have also landed her consultancy positions with major corporations, such as Knight Ridder.

Her experience, design talent, and almost-unhealthy attention to detail have ushered a flurry of clients her way, including the *New York Post* Online Store; Florida Counseling Association; photographer Robin Hill; photographer/illustrator Philip Brooker; and Maria Housden, author of *Hannah's Gift*.

A graduate of the University of Miami School of Communication, Ivonne lives in South Miami, Florida with her three cats.

Yanier Gonzalez serves as the Executive Creative Director of ModernMethod, a multitalented Web development agency in Miami that he co-founded in 1999.

As creative director, Yanier manages the development of all company projects, working hand-in-hand with clients to realize their strategic and technology goals on the Web. Some of his most notable work includes e-commerce Web sites for Atlantis Resorts of the Bahamas, Metabolic Nutrition, the *New York Post* Online Store, the Orange Bowl Committee, and for various departments at the University of Miami.

Yanier is also the creative director to Internet consulting powerhouse WWWorldmedia, where he launched successful online advertising campaigns for Hawaiian Airlines, Charles Schwab, Spirit Airlines, and Holland America. He also sits on the advisory committee of TeRespondo, a popular Latin American search engine. Previous to founding Modern Method, Yanier was the head graphic designer for TigerDirect, where his team launched the highly successful e-commerce store for the Fortune 1000 company.

A technology junkie and published writer, Yanier was the technical editor and contributing writer for *Teach Yourself Dreamweaver MX VISUALLY* and the technical editor for *Dreamweaver MX For Dummies*. An artist by training, Yanier won the prestigious 1997 *Miami Herald* Silver Knight award for art in Dade County and is a Ford Scholarship winner.

Yanier lives in Miami. He speaks fluent Spanish and can boogie on a unicycle.

COLOPHON

This book was produced electronically in Indianapolis, Indiana. Microsoft Word 2000 was used for word processing; design and layout were produced using QuarkXPress 4.11 and Adobe Photoshop 5.5 on Power Macintosh computers. The typeface families used are: Chicago Laser, Minion, Myriad, Myriad Multiple Master, Prestige Elite, Symbol, Trajan, and Zapf Dingbats.

Acquisitions Editor: **Michael Roney**
Project Editor: **Sarah Hellert**
Technical Editor: **Mary Rich**
Copy Editor: **Jerelind Charles**
Permissions Editor: **Carmen Krikorian**
Editorial Manager: **Rev Mengle**
Special Help: **Timothy J. Borek, David E. Gregory**
Wiley Technology Publishing Group: **Richard Swadley, Vice President and Executive Group Publisher; Bob Ipsen, Vice President and Executive Publisher; Barry Pruett, Vice President and Executive Publisher**
Production Coordinator: **Dale White**
Production: **Laura Albert, Beth Brooks, John Tyler Connoley, Joyce Haughey, Andy Hollandbeck, LeAndra Johnson**
Proofreading and Indexing: **Sharon Hilgenberg, Linda Quigley**

INDEX

WILEY PUBLISHING END-USER LICENSE AGREEMENT

READ THIS. You should carefully read these terms and conditions before opening the software packet(s) included with this book "Book". This is a license agreement "Agreement" between you and Wiley Publishing, Inc. "WPI". By opening the accompanying software packet(s), you acknowledge that you have read and accept the following terms and conditions. If you do not agree and do not want to be bound by such terms and conditions, promptly return the Book and the unopened software packet(s) to the place you obtained them for a full refund.

1. **License Grant.** WPI grants to you (either an individual or entity) a nonexclusive license to use one copy of the enclosed software program(s) (collectively, the "Software") solely for your own personal or business purposes on a single computer (whether a standard computer or a workstation component of a multi-user network). The Software is in use on a computer when it is loaded into temporary memory (RAM) or installed into permanent memory (hard disk, CD-ROM, or other storage device). WPI reserves all rights not expressly granted herein.

2. **Ownership.** WPI is the owner of all right, title, and interest, including copyright, in and to the compilation of the Software recorded on the disk(s) or CD-ROM "Software Media". Copyright to the individual programs recorded on the Software Media is owned by the author or other authorized copyright owner of each program. Ownership of the Software and all proprietary rights relating thereto remain with WPI and its licensers.

3. **Restrictions On Use and Transfer.**

   (a) You may only (i) make one copy of the Software for backup or archival purposes, or (ii) transfer the Software to a single hard disk, provided that you keep the original for backup or archival purposes. You may not (i) rent or lease the Software, (ii) copy or reproduce the Software through a LAN or other network system or through any computer subscriber system or bulletin-board system, or (iii) modify, adapt, or create derivative works based on the Software.

   (b) You may not reverse engineer, decompile, or disassemble the Software. You may transfer the Software and user documentation on a permanent basis, provided that the transferee agrees to accept the terms and conditions of this Agreement and you retain no copies. If the Software is an update or has been updated, any transfer must include the most recent update and all prior versions.

4. **Restrictions on Use of Individual Programs.** You must follow the individual requirements and restrictions detailed for each individual program in the About the CD-ROM appendix of this Book. These limitations are also contained in the individual license agreements recorded on the Software Media. These limitations may include a requirement that after using the program for a specified period of time, the user must pay a registration fee or discontinue use. By opening the Software packet(s), you will be agreeing to abide by the licenses and restrictions for these individual programs that are detailed in the About the CD-ROM appendix and on the Software Media. None of the material on this Software Media or listed in this Book may ever be redistributed, in original or modified form, for commercial purposes.

5. **Limited Warranty.**

   (a) WPI warrants that the Software and Software Media are free from defects in materials and workmanship under normal use for a period of sixty (60) days from the date of purchase of this Book. If WPI receives notification within the warranty period of defects in materials or workmanship, WPI will replace the defective Software Media.

   (b) WPI AND THE AUTHOR OF THE BOOK DISCLAIM ALL OTHER WARRANTIES, EXPRESS OR IMPLIED, INCLUDING WITHOUT LIMITATION IMPLIED WARRANTIES OF MERCHANTABILITY AND FITNESS FOR A PARTICULAR PURPOSE, WITH RESPECT TO THE SOFTWARE, THE PROGRAMS, THE SOURCE CODE CONTAINED THEREIN, AND/OR THE TECHNIQUES DESCRIBED IN THIS BOOK. WPI DOES NOT WARRANT THAT THE FUNCTIONS CONTAINED IN THE SOFTWARE WILL MEET YOUR REQUIREMENTS OR THAT THE OPERATION OF THE SOFTWARE WILL BE ERROR FREE.

   (c) This limited warranty gives you specific legal rights, and you may have other rights that vary from jurisdiction to jurisdiction.

6. **Remedies.**

   (a) WPI's entire liability and your exclusive remedy for defects in materials and workmanship shall be limited to replacement of the Software Media, which may be returned to WPI with a copy of your receipt at the following address: Software Media Fulfillment Department, Attn.: 50 Fast Dreamweaver MX Techniques, Wiley Publishing, Inc., 10475 Crosspoint Blvd., Indianapolis, IN 46256, or call 1-800-762-2974. Please allow four to six weeks for delivery. This Limited Warranty is void if failure of the Software Media has resulted from accident, abuse, or misapplication. Any replacement Software Media will be warranted for the remainder of the original warranty period or thirty (30) days, whichever is longer.

   (b) In no event shall WPI or the author be liable for any damages whatsoever (including without limitation damages for loss of business profits, business interruption, loss of business information, or any other pecuniary loss) arising from the use of or inability to use the Book or the Software, even if WPI has been advised of the possibility of such damages.

   (c) Because some jurisdictions do not allow the exclusion or limitation of liability for consequential or incidental damages, the above limitation or exclusion may not apply to you.

7. **U.S. Government Restricted Rights.** Use, duplication, or disclosure of the Software for or on behalf of the United States of America, its agencies and/or instrumentalities "U.S. Government" is subject to restrictions as stated in paragraph (c)(1)(ii) of the Rights in Technical Data and Computer Software clause of DFARS 252.227-7013, or subparagraphs (c) (1) and (2) of the Commercial Computer Software - Restricted Rights clause at FAR 52.227-19, and in similar clauses in the NASA FAR supplement, as applicable.

8. **General.** This Agreement constitutes the entire understanding of the parties and revokes and supersedes all prior agreements, oral or written, between them and may not be modified or amended except in a writing signed by both parties hereto that specifically refers to this Agreement. This Agreement shall take precedence over any other documents that may be in conflict herewith. If any one or more provisions contained in this Agreement are held by any court or tribunal to be invalid, illegal, or otherwise unenforceable, each and every other provision shall remain in full force and effect.